TOTS!

50 TOT-ALLY AWESOME RECIPES *from* TOTCHOS *to* SWEET PO-TOT-O PIE

DAN WHALEN
CREATOR OF THE FOOD IN MY BEARD

Workman Publishing · New York

Library of Congress Cataloging-in-Publication Data is available.

ISBN: 978-0-7611-8994-7

Design by Jean-Marc Troadec
Photography by Matthew Benson
Food stylist: Lisa Homa
Prop stylist: Sara Abalan

Workman books are available at special discounts when purchased in bulk for premiums and sales promotions as well as for fund-raising or educational use. Special editions or book excerpts can also be created to specification. For details, contact the Special Sales Director at the address below, or send an email to specialmarkets@workman.com.

Workman Publishing Co., Inc.
225 Varick Street
New York, NY 10014-4381
workman.com

WORKMAN is a registered trademark of Workman Publishing Co., Inc.

Printed in China
First printing April 2018

10 9 8 7 6 5 4 3 2 1

CONTENTS

INTRODUCTION 1

CHAPTER 1
TOTS 101: BASICS 3

CHAPTER 2
TOT'PETIZERS: SMALL BITES WITH BIG FLAVOR 21

CHAPTER 3
TOT O' THE MORNING TO YOU: TOTS AT THE BREAKFAST TABLE . . 73

CHAPTER 4
TOT-ALLY SATISFYING: TOTS IN THE MAIN ATTRACTION 95

CHAPTER 5
SWEET TOTS FOR YOUR SWEET TOOTH: TOTS DO DESSERT 131

INDEX 153

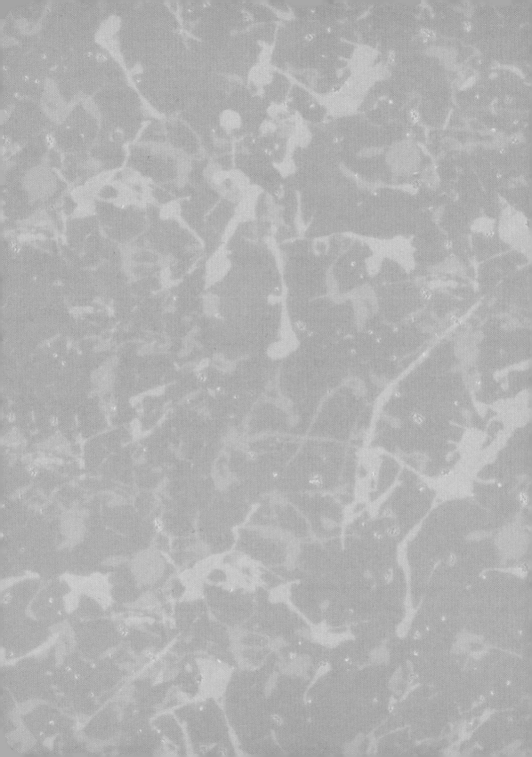

INTRODUCTION

Welcome to the wonderful world of tots! Tots are something we all grew up with, and they are making a comeback in an awesome way. When I started doing research to write this book, I discovered more and more restaurants cooking with tots, from fine-dining establishments making homemade tots with beef bacon, to hole-in-the-wall joints serving trashy loaded tots. There are a few restaurants near where I live in Boston that even specialize in these little balls of potato magic, devoting a whole section of their menus to varieties of totchos.

After my in-depth tot sleuthing, intense research, and varied samplings, I set out to write recipes that don't simply retread the same old flavors. We all know that tots taste good with cheese, and although this book does include many tasty variations on that theme, I really tried to push myself off the beaten path to develop new and unique ideas for tots. So that's why in addition to the perhaps more familiar Totchos (page 23) and Loaded Tots (page 25), you'll also find the Korean-inflected Bibimtot (page 97), Shepherd's Pie with a Totty Top (page 117), and even desserts like Salted Caramel Tot Cookies (page 147). If it tastes good with a tot, you'll find it here.

I always consider my recipes to be springboards for inspiration, so don't feel like you need to follow them precisely. If you do, these recipes are all well tested and will come out great, but if you want to swap out flavors and make them your own, more power to you! There are even a few pages dedicated just to inspiration and alternative tot twists.

Before we get into the main recipes though, we'll dive into some Tots 101 (see page 3). The world of tots is vast and varied, so read on for some tips, tricks, and foundational recipes to get you started.

CHAPTER 1

TOTS 101

THE BASICS

CHOOSING YOUR TOTS

There is an excellent recipe for homemade tots on page 9, and the best way to eat them is fresh from the fryer with a little salt and dipping sauce. But there are also more than fifty tot-centric recipes in these pages, and there's no reason *not* to use store-bought tots to make them! Commercial tots are easy, affordable, and delicious—they're pretty much the perfect food—so no need to overcomplicate things. Here's a quick cheat sheet so you know what's what in the world of tots—and in the recipes that follow:

Frozen tots: When it comes to commercial tots, there are a lot more brands out there than you might expect. Each one is a little different, and they all have pros and cons. Some fare better in the oven, while others work best in the fryer. Some are dense and others are light. Ore-Ida was the first to make tots (they even coined the name Tater Tots and trademarked it) and theirs are great, but I suggest trying as many brands as you can find before settling on a favorite. Also keep an eye on the ingredients: Some tots have added flavors like garlic, while others do not. Depending on what recipe you're making, these flavors might help or hurt the final dish. (Have you ever had onion and garlic in a dessert? Not good.) Generally speaking, in my recipes I refer to the traditionally sized, standard-issue tots as "frozen tots," and unless otherwise noted, they should be used straight from the freezer.

Mini tots: In addition to different brands, there are also different sizes and shapes. One of the hardest to find is mini tots. A few recipes call for them, but it really isn't a big deal if you can't find them (you can use regular tots instead).

Coin-shape tots: I like to use coin-shape tots (called Crispy Crowns! by the main brand that makes them—Ore-Ida again) in a handful of recipes here (see pages 47, 51, 67, 70). They are great in place of a cracker or slice of bread—essentially as a mini plate for food—

and are best pan-fried because they only have two main sides. If you can't find them, you can just use regular tots and flatten them a little bit with a spatula halfway through the cooking process.

Sweet potato tots: I also call for these in a couple of recipes, in the dessert section. Again, make sure they aren't seasoned with garlic and onion!

Monster tots: These are large breakfast tots—aka hash brown patties—the kind you see at certain fast food joints. These are usually sold in the frozen breakfast foods section near the sausage and are sometimes labeled as latkes (even though they are nothing like traditional latkes at all). These work as bread for a sandwich (see page 125) or can be topped like a pizza (see page 44).

DEFROSTING FROZEN TOTS

Most of the recipes in the book call for using frozen tots as is (i.e., straight from the freezer), but there are a handful that require defrosting the tiny taters first. It's simple: If you want the tots intact, place them on a tray and let them sit out at room temperature until they've thawed, 1 to 2 hours. If the desired result is mashed up tots, place them on a microwave-safe plate and microwave them at 1-minute intervals (working in batches if necessary), stirring between each round, until they're defrosted (they will be fragile and may fall apart a bit).

Either way, handle the thawed tots with care because they're fragile and fall apart easily.

COOKING YOUR TOTS

The packaging on your tots may be a little misleading. Some brands only give directions for baking, but the reality is all tots can be baked, fried, or even pan-fried.

Every recipe in this book sticks to one of these three methods based on the best results for that specific recipe, but feel free to switch up the method depending on your taste preferences and skill level! Deep-fried tots will almost always have the best flavor and texture, but not everyone wants to deep-fry at home. I find that pan-frying is a happy middle ground for convenience, taste, and texture, but it can be annoying when you are making more than 30 tots. In that case, the best option is usually baking. In order to master the baking method, make sure that the oven is fully preheated, the tots aren't touching one another and are lightly coated in oil, and remember to flip them halfway through cooking. Following are the basic instructions for each method, beginning with my favorite.

TO PAN-FRY TOTS

1 Heat a large frying pan over medium-high heat. Pour enough vegetable or peanut oil into the pan to coat the bottom with a thin layer. Line a plate with a paper towel.

2 Once the oil is hot and is starting to ripple in the pan, add the tots, one by one, making sure they're not touching. (You don't want to crowd the pan or the tots will be soggy and may fall apart—depending on the size of your pan, you can cook about 30 tots at a time.) Cook until crispy and well browned on the bottom, about 5 minutes.

3 Gently flip the tots to turn them browned side up. Cook until brown on the other side, about 3 minutes.

4 Cook, tossing occasionally, until browned on all sides, about 3 minutes more. Transfer them to the prepared plate and season lightly with salt. Let cool about 1 minute before serving or using as directed.

TO DEEP-FRY TOTS

1 Pour vegetable or peanut oil to a depth of 4 inches into a large, heavy-bottomed pot. Heat the oil over medium-high heat until a deep-fry or candy thermometer inserted into the oil reaches 375°F. Set a cooling rack over a layer of paper towels.

2 Use a slotted metal spoon to gently drop the tots into the oil, making sure not to crowd the pot. Be extra careful if you see any frost or ice crystals on the tots, which will cause the oil to splatter. Fry until golden brown and delicious-looking, about 3 minutes.

3 Remove the tots from the pot with the slotted spoon. Place them on the cooling rack and season lightly with salt. Let cool about 1 minute before serving or using as directed.

TO BAKE TOTS

1 Preheat the oven to 450°F.

2 Coat a rimmed baking sheet with a slick of vegetable or peanut oil, add the tots, drizzle them with additional oil (about 1½ teaspoons per 45 tots), and toss to coat them evenly. Spread the tots apart to avoid crowding the pan.

3 Bake, carefully flipping the tots halfway through, until browned and crispy, about 25 minutes (20 minutes for mini tots and coin-shape tots, 30 minutes for monster tots, aka hash brown patties). Let cool about 1 minute before serving or using as directed.

HOW TO MAKE TOTS FROM SCRATCH

Once you find your favorite brand of frozen store-bought tots and get good at cooking them just right, you may wonder why anyone would make tots from scratch. But homemade tots fresh from the fryer are a magical thing. While writing this book, I went to many restaurants that boasted homemade tots, and made many recipes I found online, but in the end I was underwhelmed. Some homemade tots were more like potato croquettes with lots of stuff mixed in; others were more like latkes with long shreds of potato that were undercooked and overcooked at the same time. The third variety of so-called homemade tots were really just mashed potatoes that had been breaded and fried.

I wanted to cut through all the madness and develop the perfect homemade tot recipe—and this is it. These are easy to make at home and the recipe just works. No egg, no flour or breadcrumbs, nothing but potatoes and some fat. The best part of making tots at home is being able to mix in other flavors.

Check out page 12 for a variety of fun flavoring options.

HOMEMADE TOTS

MAKES ABOUT 30 TOTS

- 1¼ POUNDS RUSSET POTATOES, PEELED AND CUT INTO ¼-INCH CUBES
- 2 TABLESPOONS VEGETABLE OR PEANUT OIL, PLUS EXTRA FOR FRYING
- 1 TEASPOON KOSHER SALT
- ¼ CUP POTATO FLAKES (INSTANT MASHED POTATOES)
- 2 TABLESPOONS (¼ STICK) UNSALTED BUTTER, MELTED

1 Preheat the oven to 450°F.

2 Put the potatoes in a large bowl, add the 2 tablespoons oil and ½ teaspoon of the salt, and toss well to coat. Spread the potatoes out on a rimmed baking sheet and bake until the bottoms are browned but the tops are a little undercooked, about 15 minutes. Remove from the oven and allow to cool for 10 minutes.

3 Pour oil to a depth of 4 inches into a large, heavy-bottomed pot. Heat the oil over medium-high heat until a deep-fry or candy thermometer inserted into the oil reaches 375°F.

4 In the meantime, transfer the cooled potatoes to the bowl of a food processor, along with any oil from the baking sheet, and pulse about 30 times until the potato pieces are pea-size or smaller.

5 Pour the potatoes into a large bowl, add the potato flakes, butter, and remaining ½ teaspoon salt, and stir to combine.

6 Scoop up about 2 tablespoons of the potato mixture and, using your hands, form it into a tot shape; place the formed tot on a plate or rimmed baking sheet. Repeat with the remaining potato mixture.

7 Fry the tots in batches of 10 until crispy, about 4 to 5 minutes per batch. (Make sure the oil temperature returns to 375°F before frying each additional batch.) Let drain and cool slightly on a cooling rack. Serve hot.

To bake these homemade tots instead of frying them, use a mini muffin tin. Because the tots have contact with the tin on most sides, they get nicely browned and crispy. Keep the oven on after baking the potatoes in step 2. Grease the cups of the mini muffin tin with oil and pack 2 tablespoons of the tot mixture into the bottom of each to make coin-shape tots. Bake at 450°F until crisp on the bottom and sides, about 20 minutes.

VEGGIE TOTS

When making tots with a vegetable that isn't a potato, the main concern is starch content—other veggies have much less starch, meaning they're more likely to break down and fall apart in the fryer. Although I steer clear of using egg and breadcrumbs as a binder in my potato tots, with other veggies you need those (and some potato flakes) to keep everything intact.

VEGETABLE OR PEANUT OIL,
FOR FRYING

2 TABLESPOONS (¼ STICK)
UNSALTED BUTTER, MELTED

1 LARGE EGG

¼ CUP PANKO BREADCRUMBS

½ CUP POTATO FLAKES (INSTANT
MASHED POTATOES)

PREPARED VEGGIES
(SEE VEGGIE VARIATIONS)

1 CUP (4 OUNCES) FRESHLY
SHREDDED CHEDDAR CHEESE
(OPTIONAL, BUT DELICIOUS)

1 Pour oil to a depth of 4 inches into a large, heavy-bottomed pot. Heat over medium-high heat until a deep-fry or candy thermometer inserted into the oil reaches 375°F. Set a cooling rack over a layer of paper towels.

2 Whisk together the melted butter, egg, breadcrumbs, and potato flakes in a large bowl. Add the prepared veggies and the cheese, if using, and stir to incorporate.

3 Scoop up about 2 tablespoons of the veggie mixture and, using your hands, form it into a tot shape; place the formed tot on a plate or baking sheet. Repeat with the remaining potato mixture.

4 Fry the tots in batches of 10 until crispy, 4 to 5 minutes per batch. Transfer to the cooling rack and let drain and cool slightly. Serve hot. (Alternatively, bake the tots using the method on page 9.)

VEGGIE VARIATIONS

Each of the following variations begins with 1 pound cleaned or peeled raw vegetable(s), chopped into ¾-inch cubes. Feel free to use these vegetables individually or in combination.

Broccoli or Cauliflower: Toss the cubed vegetables on a baking sheet with vegetable or peanut oil and roast at 450°F until tender and browned at the edges, about 12 minutes. Let cool, then pulse in the bowl of a food processor until all the pieces are pea-size or smaller.

Sweet Potatoes or Beets: Toss the cubed vegetables on a baking sheet with vegetable or peanut oil and bake at 400°F until tender and browned at the edges, about 18 minutes. Let cool, then pulse in the bowl of a food processor until all the pieces are pea-size or smaller.

Zucchini or Apples: Pulse the cubed vegetables or fruit in the bowl of a food processor until all the pieces are pea-size or smaller.

FLAVOR BOOSTERS

To make any of these variations, follow the tot recipe on page 9, and add these ingredient combinations before you form and fry (or bake) the tots.

SIMPLE FLAVOR BOOST: Many store-bought tots have garlic and onion powder built in. Let's take it one level further. Stir 1 teaspoon garlic powder, 1 teaspoon onion powder, 1 teaspoon paprika, and ½ teaspoon dried oregano into the potato mixture in step 5.

CORNED BEEF HASH TOTS: If you make these and use them in the Tots Benedict on page 77, breakfast will never be the same. Stir 1 large egg, 3 ounces cooked and finely chopped or shredded corned beef, and 2 additional tablespoons potato flakes into the potato mixture in step 5.

VINDALOO TOTS: An Indian twist on tots. Before preheating the oven in step 1, make caramelized onions: Sauté 1 medium onion, diced, in 1 teaspoon vegetable or peanut oil in a large frying pan over low heat, stirring occasionally, until the onion is evenly browned, about 25 minutes. Let cool.

In step 5, add 1 large egg, 2 tablespoons caramelized onions, 2 teaspoons curry powder, ½ teaspoon garlic powder, ½ teaspoon ground ginger, and an additional 1 tablespoon potato flakes to the potato mixture.

BAKED POTATO TOTS: Bacon makes everything better. Including tots. To the potato mixture in step 5, add 1 large egg; 3 bacon strips, cooked and crumbled; 2 tablespoons chopped fresh chives; ½ cup (2 ounces) freshly shredded Cheddar cheese; and an additional 1 tablespoon potato flakes.

TACO TOTS: Taco flavors built right into the tots—cheese and everything! In step 5, stir into the potato mixture 1 large egg; 3 ounces ground beef, cooked and crumbled; 1 teaspoon ground cumin; 1 teaspoon paprika; 1 teaspoon ground chipotle; ½ teaspoon ground coriander; ½ cup (2 ounces) freshly shredded Cheddar cheese; and an additional 1 tablespoon potato flakes.

Remove from the food processor and put into a mesh strainer. Mix in ½ teaspoon salt. Set the strainer over a large bowl (or the sink) and allow to drain for 1 hour. Place the zucchini or apples in a clean kitchen towel or cheesecloth and wring out the excess liquid before using.

SIMPLE SEASONINGS, SAUCES, AND DIPS

These seasoning remixes offer some easy ways to jazz up basic tots. Before spicing the tots, note that you'll first want to cook them using your preferred method—pan-frying (page 7), deep-frying (page 8), or baking (page 8). And make sure the tots are fresh from the heat and piping hot when you add the seasonings.

Another way to class up your store-bought tots is by serving them alongside a homemade dipping sauce. All of the recipes on pages 16–19 are really great, but the onion dip will change your life.

ROSEMARY TRUFFLE TOTS

We all love truffle fries, so why not truffle tots? I like mine with fresh rosemary to add a subtle piney flavor to balance the earthy truffle.

MAKES 30 TOTS

1 TABLESPOON TRUFFLE OIL

2 TEASPOONS CHOPPED FRESH ROSEMARY LEAVES

KOSHER SALT AND FRESHLY GROUND BLACK PEPPER

30 VERY HOT, FRESHLY COOKED TOTS

Stir together the truffle oil, rosemary, and salt and pepper to taste in a small bowl. Place the tots in a medium-size bowl and drizzle with the oil mixture. Toss gently to coat the tots, being careful not to break them. Serve hot.

CACIO E PEPE TOTS

Cacio e pepe is a classic Italian pasta preparation in which you toss long pasta (like spaghetti) with cheese and black pepper until a luscious sauce forms and clings to the noodles. Doing the same thing with tots won't exactly form a sauce, but the cheese and pepper stick to the crispy tots nicely and the flavor is out of this world.

Make sure you grate the cheese with a Microplane (or the smallest holes on a box grater, if you don't have one) so that it's feathery and ready to hug the tots.

MAKES 30 TOTS

30 VERY HOT, FRESHLY COOKED TOTS

2 CUPS FINELY GRATED, VERY LOOSELY PACKED PECORINO ROMANO CHEESE (SEE HEADNOTE)

½ TABLESPOON FRESHLY GROUND BLACK PEPPER (I LIKE FINELY GROUND FOR THIS, BUT IT'S UP TO YOU)

Place the tots in a medium-size bowl and immediately top with the cheese and black pepper. Toss gently to coat the tots, being careful not to break them. (You will see the cheese dissolve into a coating for the tots fairly quickly.) Serve hot.

GARLIC AND CHIVE TOTS

G arlic and chives are a classic pairing with potatoes and even a common potato chip flavor. This version uses fresh garlic and chives for that added punch of homemade goodness.

MAKES 30 TOTS

½ GARLIC CLOVE, GRATED ON A MICROPLANE GRATER OR CRUSHED IN A PRESS

½ TABLESPOON CHOPPED FRESH CHIVES

1 TABLESPOON OLIVE OIL

KOSHER SALT AND FRESHLY GROUND BLACK PEPPER

30 VERY HOT, FRESHLY COOKED TOTS

Stir together the garlic, chives, oil, and salt and pepper to taste in a small bowl. Place the tots in a medium-size bowl and drizzle with the garlic mixture. Toss gently to coat the tots, being careful not to break them. Serve hot.

SESAME GINGER TOTS

A little Asian flair with a kick of heat make for unexpectedly delicious tots.

MAKES 30 TOTS

2 TEASPOONS GROUND GINGER

2 TEASPOONS CRUSHED RED PEPPER FLAKES

1 TEASPOON SESAME SEEDS

1 TABLESPOON TOASTED SESAME OIL

KOSHER SALT AND FRESHLY GROUND BLACK PEPPER

30 VERY HOT, FRESHLY COOKED TOTS

Stir together the ginger, red pepper flakes, sesame seeds, oil, and salt and pepper to taste in a small bowl. Place the tots in a medium-size bowl and drizzle with the ginger mixture. Toss gently to coat the tots, being careful not to break them. Serve hot.

CHIPOTLE MAYO

T his dipping sauce is spicy, tangy, and a little sweet—and takes only a few minutes to put together. Serve it with plain cooked tots, or try it on the side with the Bacon-Wrapped Tots on page 42.

MAKES ABOUT 1 CUP

¼ CUP MAYONNAISE

¼ CUP SOUR CREAM

2 TEASPOONS BROWN SUGAR

1 TEASPOON RED WINE VINEGAR

LEAVES FROM 2 SPRIGS FRESH OREGANO (OR 1 TEASPOON DRIED OREGANO)

1 CHIPOTLE PEPPER IN ADOBO SAUCE, PLUS 1 TABLESPOON ADOBO SAUCE FROM THE CAN

Combine all of the ingredients in the bowl of a food processor and pulse until smooth.

Chipotle Mayo will keep, in an airtight container in the refrigerator, for up to 3 days.

SPICY CHEESE SAUCE

T his isn't some fancy roux-based cheese sauce, it's the bright yellow kind you might find served on nachos at a baseball game. It doesn't get better than dipping your tots in this—or dumping it on top of them.

MAKES ABOUT 1½ CUPS

1 CUP WHOLE MILK

1 CUP NONFAT DRY MILK POWDER

1 TABLESPOON CORNSTARCH

1 BLOCK (8 OUNCES) CHEDDAR CHEESE, FRESHLY SHREDDED (SEE NOTE)

1 TEASPOON HOT SAUCE

¼ CUP DICED PICKLED JALAPEÑOS

2 TEASPOONS CRUSHED RED PEPPER FLAKES

1 Combine the milk, milk powder, and cornstarch in a large, heavy-bottomed pot over medium heat and bring to a simmer, whisking constantly. Continue to cook, whisking, until the sauce thickens and the milk powder has dissolved, about 1 minute.

2 Remove from the heat and whisk in the cheese. The cheese should melt, no problem, but if it doesn't, return the pot to low heat and whisk until it does. (Be careful with the heat at this point because the sauce could separate if heated too rapidly.)

3 Allow the cheese sauce to cool slightly, then stir in the hot sauce, jalapeños, and red pepper flakes. Serve warm.

NOTE: Resist the temptation to use preshredded cheese here. Yes, it's easier, but it won't work in this recipe.

ONION DIP

This is the best onion dip of all time. It takes a long time to caramelize the onions perfectly, but it's totally worth it! Make this once and you will be making it for every party you have for the rest of your life. *MAKES 2 CUPS*

4 TABLESPOONS (½ STICK) UNSALTED BUTTER

2 LARGE YELLOW ONIONS, DICED

2 LARGE WHITE ONIONS, DICED

KOSHER SALT

½ CUP MAYONNAISE

⅓ CUP SOUR CREAM

⅓ CUP PLAIN FULL-FAT YOGURT, PLUS EXTRA AS NEEDED

½ GARLIC CLOVE

1 BUNCH (1 OUNCE) FRESH CHIVES, FINELY CHOPPED (ABOUT ¾ CUP)

1 TEASPOON PAPRIKA, PLUS EXTRA AS NEEDED

1 TEASPOON FRESHLY GROUND BLACK PEPPER, PLUS EXTRA AS NEEDED

JUICE OF 1 LEMON, PLUS EXTRA AS NEEDED

HOT SAUCE (OPTIONAL)

1 Place the butter in a large, heavy-bottomed frying pan over medium heat. When it begins to melt, add the onions and a couple of good pinches of salt. Cook, stirring frequently and alternating the heat between medium and low as needed to avoid burning, until the onions are dark brown and reduced in volume to 1 cup, 45 minutes to 1 hour. Make sure to scrape the bottom of the pan regularly to prevent the browned bits from sticking. Remove from the heat and let cool slightly.

2 Combine the mayonnaise, sour cream, and yogurt in a medium-size bowl. Stir in the onions. Grate the garlic into the bowl, add the chives, and stir well. Add the paprika, ½ teaspoon of salt, pepper, and lemon juice and stir to incorporate. If you like, add in a few shakes of hot sauce.

3 Refrigerate, covered, for 1 hour. Uncover it, stir it up, and taste it. Is it too thick? Add a little yogurt. Adjust the seasonings as needed by adding more hot sauce (if using), lemon juice, salt, pepper, and/or paprika.

Onion Dip will keep, in an airtight container in the refrigerator, for up to 3 days.

CHIMICHURRI

I love this herby South American sauce on steak, grilled chicken, and pizza, but never thought to serve it with tots until recently. Potatoes go well with herbs, olive oil, and garlic, so the combo was a big hit.

MAKES ABOUT 1 CUP

1 BUNCH (2 OUNCES) FRESH ITALIAN (FLAT-LEAF) PARSLEY (STEMS AND ALL)

1 BUNCH (1 OUNCE) FRESH BASIL, LEAVES ONLY

1 HANDFUL FRESH OREGANO LEAVES

1 BUNCH (1 OUNCE) FRESH CHIVES

½ GARLIC CLOVE, GRATED

JUICE OF 1 LEMON

¼ CUP EXTRA VIRGIN OLIVE OIL, PLUS EXTRA FOR STORING

KOSHER SALT AND FRESHLY GROUND BLACK PEPPER

Combine the parsley, basil, oregano, chives, garlic, lemon juice, the ¼ cup olive oil, and a pinch each of salt and pepper in the bowl of a food processor or a blender and process until smooth. Serve immediately.

Chimichurri will keep, covered with a layer of olive oil and stored in an airtight container in the refrigerator, for up to 2 days.

HORSERADISH SAUCE

This classic steak sauce works great as a dipping sauce for some freshly cooked tots, and it really shines when paired with the roast beef on a tot canapé (see box on page 47). *MAKES 1 CUP*

~~~~~~~~~~~~~~~~~~~~~~~~

½ CUP SOUR CREAM

¼ CUP PREPARED HORSERADISH

2 TABLESPOONS CHOPPED FRESH ITALIAN (FLAT-LEAF) PARSLEY

1 TABLESPOON DIJON MUSTARD

1 TEASPOON FRESH LEMON JUICE

Combine all of the ingredients in a small bowl and whisk until smooth. Refrigerate, covered, to let the flavors meld, at least 2 hours.

Horseradish Sauce will keep in an airtight container in the refrigerator, for up to 2 days.

CHAPTER 2

TOT'PETIZERS

SMALL BITES WITH BIG FLAVOR

TOTCHOS

This is it—the dish that started the tot renaissance. A few years back, totchos began popping up on menus across the country, and since then it's been tot mania. Making your own pico de gallo and guac will always make this recipe special, but feel free to use store-bought. You can bake the tots for this recipe if you like, but I recommend pan-frying them—it takes this dish to the next level! For other totcho ideas, see the box on page 33. *SERVES 4*

FOR THE PICO DE GALLO

3 VINE-RIPENED TOMATOES, DICED

1 SMALL ONION, DICED

5 JALAPEÑOS, STEMMED, SEEDED IF YOU WISH TO REDUCE THE HEAT, AND DICED

1 SMALL GARLIC CLOVE, MINCED OR GRATED

½ CUP CHOPPED FRESH CILANTRO LEAVES

JUICE OF 1 LIME

KOSHER SALT

FOR THE GUACAMOLE

1 LARGE AVOCADO, HALVED AND PITTED

2 TABLESPOONS PICO DE GALLO

JUICE OF 1 LIME

KOSHER SALT

FOR THE TOTCHOS

¼ CUP VEGETABLE OR PEANUT OIL

1½ POUNDS FROZEN TOTS (ABOUT 65 TOTS)

1½ CUPS (6 OUNCES) SHREDDED CHEDDAR CHEESE

¼ CUP PICKLED SLICED JALAPEÑOS

½ CUP SOUR CREAM

1 Make the pico de gallo: Combine the tomatoes, onion, diced jalapeños, garlic, and cilantro in a small bowl. Add the lime juice and the salt to taste. Cover and refrigerate the pico de gallo until ready to use (up to 3 days).

2 Make the guacamole: Scoop the avocado into a medium-size bowl and mash with a fork. Add 2 tablespoons of the pico, along with the lime juice. Stir and add salt to taste. Cover with plastic wrap touching the surface of the guacamole and refrigerate until ready to use (up to 1 day).

3 Make the totchos: Preheat the oven to 400°F. Line a plate with paper towels.

4 Heat the oil in a 10-inch cast-iron skillet over medium-high heat and swirl to coat. Add the tots to the skillet in batches of about 20, so as not to crowd the pan, and cook, undisturbed, until browned on the bottom, about 3 minutes. Gently stir and toss the tots, being careful not to break them, until they are browned on all sides and crispy, about 10 minutes. Transfer the cooked tots to the prepared plate and repeat with the remaining tots.

5 When the final batch of tots is just about browned, pile the rest of the cooked tots back into the skillet. Top evenly with the cheese and pickled jalapeños and transfer the skillet to the oven. Bake until the cheese is melted, about 10 minutes.

6 Remove the skillet from the oven and top the totchos with the pico, guac, and sour cream. Serve immediately right in the skillet with a big serving spoon and plates and forks for everyone to dig in. Remember that the skillet is hot!

VARIATION:

To scale this recipe up for a crowd, double the pico de gallo and guacamole. Use 4 pounds of tots and divide them between 2 sheet pans (18" x 13"). Bake as directed on page 8. Continue with the recipe from step 5, doubling the cheese, pickled jalapeños, and sour cream. Follow the assembly and cooking instructions above, then dump one of the trays onto the other to form a pile. Continue with the instructions in step 5.

LOADED TOTS

For me, the main difference between Totchos (page 23) and Loaded Tots is the cheese sauce. While Totchos are baked with shredded cheese on top, Loaded Tots are smothered in a luxurious, creamy, cheesy sauce. Some bacon, sour cream, and chives come together to give them that "loaded baked potato" taste. *SERVES 4*

1 TABLESPOON VEGETABLE OR PEANUT OIL

½ POUND BACON, ROUGHLY CHOPPED

1½ POUNDS FROZEN TOTS (ABOUT 65 TOTS)

1 CUP MILK

1 CUP NONFAT DRY MILK POWDER

1 TABLESPOON CORNSTARCH

1 BLOCK (8 OUNCES) CHEDDAR CHEESE, SHREDDED (SEE NOTE)

½ CUP CHOPPED FRESH CHIVES

¼ CUP SOUR CREAM

1 Line a plate with paper towels. Heat the oil in a 10-inch cast-iron skillet over medium-high heat. Add the bacon and cook, stirring occasionally, until crispy, about 7 minutes. Use a slotted spoon to transfer the bacon to the prepared plate; reserve 2 tablespoons of the fat in the skillet.

2 Line another plate with paper towels. Add the tots to the skillet in batches of about 20, so as not to crowd the pan, and cook undisturbed until brown on the bottom, about 3 minutes. Gently stir and toss the tots, being careful not to break them, and continue to cook until they are browned on all sides and crispy, about 10 minutes. Transfer the cooked tots to the prepared plate and repeat with the remaining tots.

3 Meanwhile, whisk the milk, milk powder, and cornstarch together in a medium-size, heavy-bottomed pot over low heat. Bring to a simmer and cook, whisking, just until the milk powder is dissolved and the sauce thickens, 7 to 10 minutes. Remove from the heat.

4 Whisk the cheese into the sauce. It should melt, no problem, but you might need to set the pot over low heat briefly. Be careful with the heat at this point because the sauce could separate if it is heated too rapidly.

5 Return all of the cooked tots to the skillet, piling them up. Dump the cheese sauce on top, then sprinkle on the bacon and chives, and dot the top with the sour cream. Serve immediately.

NOTE: You'll need to freshly shred the cheese from a block. Preshredded cheese won't work as well for this recipe because it has additives that prevent it from melting smoothly.

TOTS POUTINE

I don't think I need to tell you how popular poutine has become in America over the past few years. I knew I had to include a tot version in the book. I did *very* difficult research trying poutines all across Boston, and decided that nothing beats the classic version—fried potatoes (in this case, tots) topped with gravy and cheese. *SERVES 2 OR 3*

1 POUND FROZEN TOTS
(ABOUT 45 TOTS)

1 TABLESPOON VEGETABLE OR
PEANUT OIL

2 TABLESPOONS (¼ STICK)
UNSALTED BUTTER

1 SHALLOT, MINCED

3 TABLESPOONS ALL-PURPOSE
FLOUR

2 CUPS BEEF STOCK

½ TEASPOON DRIED THYME

1 TABLESPOON WORCESTERSHIRE
SAUCE

4 OUNCES (1 HEAPING CUP) CHEESE
CURDS, AT ROOM TEMPERATURE
(SEE NOTE)

1 Preheat the oven to 450°F.

2 Place the tots on a rimmed baking sheet and drizzle them with the oil. Toss the tots gently to coat them evenly with the oil, then spread them out in an even layer. Bake, carefully flipping the tots halfway through, until they are browned evenly and crispy, about 20 minutes.

3 Meanwhile, melt the butter in a medium-size skillet over medium heat, add the shallot, and cook, stirring often, until lightly browned, about 10 minutes. Add the flour and whisk well to break up any lumps. Cook, stirring occasionally, until the flour darkens slightly in color, about 3 minutes. Whisk in the stock until smooth. Add the thyme and Worcestershire sauce and bring to a strong simmer, whisking often, until the gravy thickens, about 5 minutes. Turn the heat down very low and cover until ready to use.

4 Place your cooked tots on a plate or in a bowl. Top with the curds and then pour on the gravy. Eat immediately to prevent the tots from becoming too soggy.

NOTE: If you can't find cheese curds at your grocery store, any fresh or young cheese will work. Ask someone working at the cheese counter what might be a good substitute. I have used queso blanco, halloumi, and even string cheese in the past with good results! Also remember the cheese should be at room temperature, so remove it from the fridge before you start cooking and break it up as needed so it has time to warm up.

PUT AN EGG ON IT!

Almost any recipe in the world could benefit from a fried egg on top, and this is definitely one of them. The runny yolk takes the whole poutine experience up a notch—give it a try!

BUFFALO TOTS

When I first dreamed up this recipe, I thought of tossing the tots in the Buffalo sauce, but as I learned over and over while writing this book, tots get soggy quickly. Instead, I opted for drizzling the Buffalo sauce on top of the tots rather than coating them in it. This way you still get that addictive tot crunch with delicious Buffalo sauce flavor. *SERVES 2 OR 3*

1 POUND FROZEN TOTS
(ABOUT 45 TOTS)

2 TABLESPOONS VEGETABLE OR
PEANUT OIL

1/4 CUP CAYENNE PEPPER HOT
SAUCE (SUCH AS FRANK'S
REDHOT)

4 TABLESPOONS (1/2 STICK)
UNSALTED BUTTER, MELTED

1 TABLESPOON APPLE CIDER
VINEGAR

2 TEASPOONS WORCESTERSHIRE
SAUCE

2 OUNCES CRUMBLED BLUE CHEESE,
(ABOUT 1/2 CUP)

1/4 CUP DICED CELERY

1/4 CUP DICED CARROT

1 Preheat the oven to 450°F.

2 Place the tots on a rimmed baking sheet and drizzle them with the oil. Toss to coat evenly with the oil, then spread them out in an even layer. Bake, carefully flipping the tots halfway through, until they are browned evenly and crispy, 20 to 25 minutes.

3 Meanwhile, stir together the hot sauce, melted butter, vinegar, and Worcestershire sauce in a small bowl.

4 Pile the tots on a large plate and drizzle most of the Buffalo sauce over them to coat evenly (be careful not to drown them!). Sprinkle the blue cheese, celery, and carrot evenly on top of the coated tots.

5 Serve immediately, with the remaining Buffalo sauce in a small bowl for dipping the bottom layer of tots.

PA-TOT-AS BRAVAS

Patatas bravas is a traditional Spanish tapas dish of roasted potatoes topped with a savory tomato sauce and a rich aioli. It's sort of the Spanish equivalent of dipping your french fries into a combo of ketchup and mayo! I thought swapping out the roasted potatoes for tots would be a fun twist on this classic dish and it actually works great. The tots, as always, retain that super crispy texture and add a whole new dimension to the dish. Cook the tots in duck fat to add another level of authenticity. *SERVES 2 OR 3*

FOR THE TOMATO SAUCE

¼ CUP OLIVE OIL

1 SMALL ONION, DICED

2 GARLIC CLOVES, FINELY DICED

1 CAN (14 OUNCES) DICED TOMATOES WITH THEIR JUICES

1 TABLESPOON SMOKED PAPRIKA, PLUS EXTRA FOR GARNISH

FOR THE AIOLI

1 LARGE EGG YOLK (THE VERY FRESHEST YOU CAN FIND)

1 TEASPOON DIJON MUSTARD

½ GARLIC CLOVE, GRATED ON A MICROPLANE

½ CUP OLIVE OIL

JUICE OF ½ LEMON, PLUS EXTRA AS NEEDED

FOR THE TOTS

2 TABLESPOONS DUCK FAT (SEE NOTE) OR VEGETABLE OIL

1 POUND FROZEN TOTS (ABOUT 45 TOTS)

CHOPPED FRESH ITALIAN (FLAT-LEAF) PARSLEY, FOR GARNISH

1 Make the tomato sauce: Heat the ¼ cup of olive oil in a small saucepan over medium heat. Add the onion and cook, stirring occasionally, until lightly browned, about 10 minutes. Add the garlic and cook until fragrant and lightly golden, about 1 minute. Next add the tomatoes and their juices and the paprika and stir to combine. Puree the sauce with a stick blender (or carefully transfer it to the bowl of a food processor and process until smooth). Set aside and keep warm.

2 Make the aioli: Combine the egg yolk, mustard, and garlic in a medium-size bowl and whisk together until incorporated. Add the ½ cup olive oil in very small increments, about a teaspoon at a time, whisking well with each addition. Whisk in the lemon juice. If the aioli is too thick (it should have the consistency of a runny mayonnaise), whisk in a little more lemon juice, or a splash of water, as needed.

3 Make the tots: Line a plate with paper towels. Heat the duck fat or vegetable oil in a large frying pan over medium-high heat. When it has melted, add the tots and cook, flipping occasionally, until they are browned evenly and crispy, about 3 minutes per side. Remove the tots from the pan and let drain on the prepared plate.

4 Pile the tots on a plate and top with the tomato sauce and aioli. Garnish with a sprinkling of paprika and some chopped parsley and serve immediately.

NOTE: Duck fat can be purchased at a butcher shop or upscale grocery store.

OTHER TOT TOPPINGS

SOUTHERN BARBECUE TOTS
Pulled pork, coleslaw

COUNTRY-FRIED TOTS
Sausage gravy, egg over easy

CHILI CHEESE TOTS
Chili, grated Cheddar cheese, sour cream, chopped scallions

BANH MI TOTS
Barbecued pulled pork, pickled carrot and daikon, sriracha mayo, chopped fresh cilantro, fried egg

PIZZA TOTS
Tomato sauce, shredded mozzarella, pepperoni slices

GREEK TOTS
Tzatziki, cooked ground lamb, kalamata olives, chopped fresh parsley

STROGANOFF TOTS
Sauteed mushrooms and onions, shaved steak, sour cream, parsley

GRILLED BEEF TOTS
Sliced steak, pickle slices, chopped fresh parsley

CHEESESTEAK TOTS
Shaved beef, caramelized onions, Cheez Whiz, chopped banana peppers

REUBEN TOTS
Corned beef, sliced Swiss cheese, sauerkraut, Thousand Island dressing

CHEESEBURGER TOTS
Cooked ground beef, American cheese, ketchup, mustard, pickle slices, shredded lettuce

SLOPPY TOTS
Sloppy joe filling, American cheese

CHOWDER TOTS
New England clam chowder

TOTS BOLOGNESE
Bolognese sauce, shredded mozzarella and Parmesan cheeses, marinated mushrooms

LOBSTER ROLL TOTS
Fresh lobster meat lightly dressed with mayo, chopped celery, chopped fresh chives

TOT CAESAR

Caesar salad is one of those dishes that people fuss over and take so seriously, but it's actually very easy to get right. You only need a few things: egg yolks, olive oil, Parmesan cheese, romaine lettuce, and of course some crunchy croutons. This version obviously swaps out the croutons for crispy tots. Mini tots work best in this recipe, but the standard-size ones are yummy, too.

MAKES 3 LARGE SALADS; SERVES 3 TO 6

45 FROZEN MINI TOTS
(OR 30 STANDARD-SIZE TOTS)

¼ CUP OLIVE OIL, PLUS
1 TABLESPOON FOR COATING
THE TOTS

3 ANCHOVIES PACKED IN OLIVE OIL
(FROM A JAR OR TIN), DRAINED

KOSHER SALT

1 TEASPOON DIJON MUSTARD

1 LARGE EGG YOLK (THE VERY
FRESHEST YOU CAN FIND)

JUICE OF 1 LEMON

1 TEASPOON WORCESTERSHIRE
SAUCE

3 ROMAINE HEARTS, CORES
REMOVED AND LEAVES CHOPPED
INTO BITE-SIZE PIECES
(OR LEFT WHOLE IF YOU
WANT TO BE HIP ABOUT IT)

⅓ CUP FRESHLY GRATED
PARMESAN CHEESE

FRESHLY CRACKED BLACK PEPPER

1 Preheat the oven to 450°F.

2 Place the tots on a rimmed baking sheet and drizzle them with 1 tablespoon of olive oil. Toss the tots gently to coat them evenly with the oil, then spread them out in an even layer.

Bake, carefully flipping the tots halfway through, until they are browned evenly and crispy, about 20 minutes (25 minutes for standard-size tots).

3 Place the anchovies in a large bowl, add a pinch of salt, and mash up with a fork. Whisk in the mustard and egg yolk until combined. Very slowly, start adding ¼ cup of olive oil, beginning with a couple of teaspoons and whisking it in until it is incorporated. Continue adding the oil in small increments, whisking after each addition, until all the oil is mixed in. Whisk in the lemon juice and Worcestershire sauce until combined.

4 Add the lettuce to the dressing in the bowl and toss to coat well. Divide the dressed lettuce among plates, top each with some of the Parmesan cheese, a ton of freshly cracked black pepper, and a third of the tots. Serve immediately.

TOTS A LA HUANCAINA

This Peruvian potato salad was one of my first forays into South American cuisine. I knew it would lend itself well to tots because it is basically potatoes doused in a spicy, cheesy sauce—and who doesn't like tots in a spicy, cheesy sauce? The sauce is also easy to make because it doesn't require any heating or a roux—it's all done in the blender! SERVES 3

1 POUND FROZEN TOTS
(ABOUT 45 TOTS)

1 TABLESPOON VEGETABLE OR
PEANUT OIL

½ CUP EVAPORATED MILK, PLUS
MORE AS NEEDED

10 OUNCES QUESO FRESCO CHEESE

1 PICKLED AJI AMARILLO PEPPER,
STEMMED AND SEEDED
(SEE NOTE)

1 GARLIC CLOVE, MINCED

JUICE OF 1 LIME

15 KALAMATA OLIVES, PITTED AND
ROUGHLY CHOPPED

3 LARGE HARD-BOILED EGGS,
PEELED, AND ROUGHLY CHOPPED

¼ CUP CHOPPED FRESH ITALIAN
(FLAT-LEAF) PARSLEY

1 Preheat the oven to 450°F.

2 Place the tots on a rimmed baking sheet and drizzle them with the oil. Toss the tots gently to coat them evenly with the oil, then spread them out in an even layer. Bake, carefully flipping the tots halfway through, until they are browned evenly and crispy, about 20 minutes.

3 Meanwhile, in a blender or the bowl of a food processor, combine ½ cup of evaporated milk with the cheese, pepper, garlic, and lime juice and blend on medium-high until smooth. Add more evaporated

milk if needed to thin it out (it should have the consistency of a thick sour cream or cheese sauce).

4 Spread the tots out on a platter and pour the cheesy sauce over them. Top with the chopped olives, eggs, and parsley. Serve immediately.

NOTE: Aji amarillo peppers are common in Peruvian cooking and add a unique flavor to this sauce. You can find them at many metropolitan grocery stores, or at a Peruvian market. If you can't find them, use a pickled cherry pepper instead.

NOT YOUR AUNT SANDY'S PO-TOT-O SALAD

I thought for a while how I would go about making a potato salad with tots. I was worried the cold tots would be unappetizing and fall apart. I decided my first test would be my mom's exact potato salad using tots instead of potatoes. It came out so well I wondered why I'd ever been worried. *SERVES 8 TO 10*

2 POUNDS FROZEN TOTS (ABOUT 90 TOTS)

2 TABLESPOONS VEGETABLE OR PEANUT OIL

½ CUP MAYONNAISE

¼ CUP YELLOW MUSTARD

¼ CUP PICKLE JUICE

¼ CUP APPLE CIDER VINEGAR

2 TABLESPOONS HOT SAUCE (OPTIONAL)

4 HARD-BOILED LARGE EGGS, PEELED AND CHOPPED

½ LARGE GREEN BELL PEPPER, STEMMED, SEEDED, AND DICED

½ MEDIUM ONION, DICED

4 PICKLE SPEARS, OR 1 WHOLE LARGE PICKLE, DICED

1 TABLESPOON CHOPPED FRESH DILL

1 Preheat the oven to 450°F.

2 Place the tots on a rimmed baking sheet (or two) and drizzle them with the oil. Toss the tots gently to coat them evenly with the oil, then spread them out in an even layer.

3 Bake, carefully flipping the tots halfway through, until they are browned evenly and crispy, about 25 minutes. Let cool on the baking sheet for 5 minutes.

4 Meanwhile, stir together the mayonnaise, mustard, pickle juice, vinegar, and hot sauce (if using) in a medium-size bowl.

5 When the tots are done, transfer them to a large bowl. Add the chopped egg, all the veggies, the mayonnaise sauce, and the dill. Stir to combine.

6 Cover with plastic wrap and refrigerate for a few hours to chill before serving.

Not Your Aunt Sandy's Po-tot-o Salad will keep, in an airtight container in the refrigerator, for 3 days.

BACON-WRAPPED TOTS

Dress up your tots in a bacon suit. For some reason, wrapping tots in bacon makes them feel fancy (it also makes them delicious). You could serve these as passed hors d'oeuvre at the most elegant party, or just whip up a batch to devour at your next game night (the recipe scales up easily). I highly recommend serving these with the Chipotle Mayo on page 16 or the Horseradish Sauce on page 19. *SERVES 5*

24 FROZEN TOTS

12 BACON STRIPS

DIPPING SAUCE(S) OF YOUR CHOICE, FOR SERVING

1 Preheat the oven to 425°F. Set a wire rack on a rimmed baking sheet.

2 Cut the bacon strips in half crosswise. Wrap a piece of bacon around each tot and place each, seam-side down, on the rack.

3 Bake until the tots are browned and the bacon is cooked through and crispy, about 25 minutes. (The cooking time will vary depending on the thickness of the bacon, so keep your eyes on them!)

4 Transfer the tots to a platter, skewer each with a toothpick, and serve immediately with the dipping sauce.

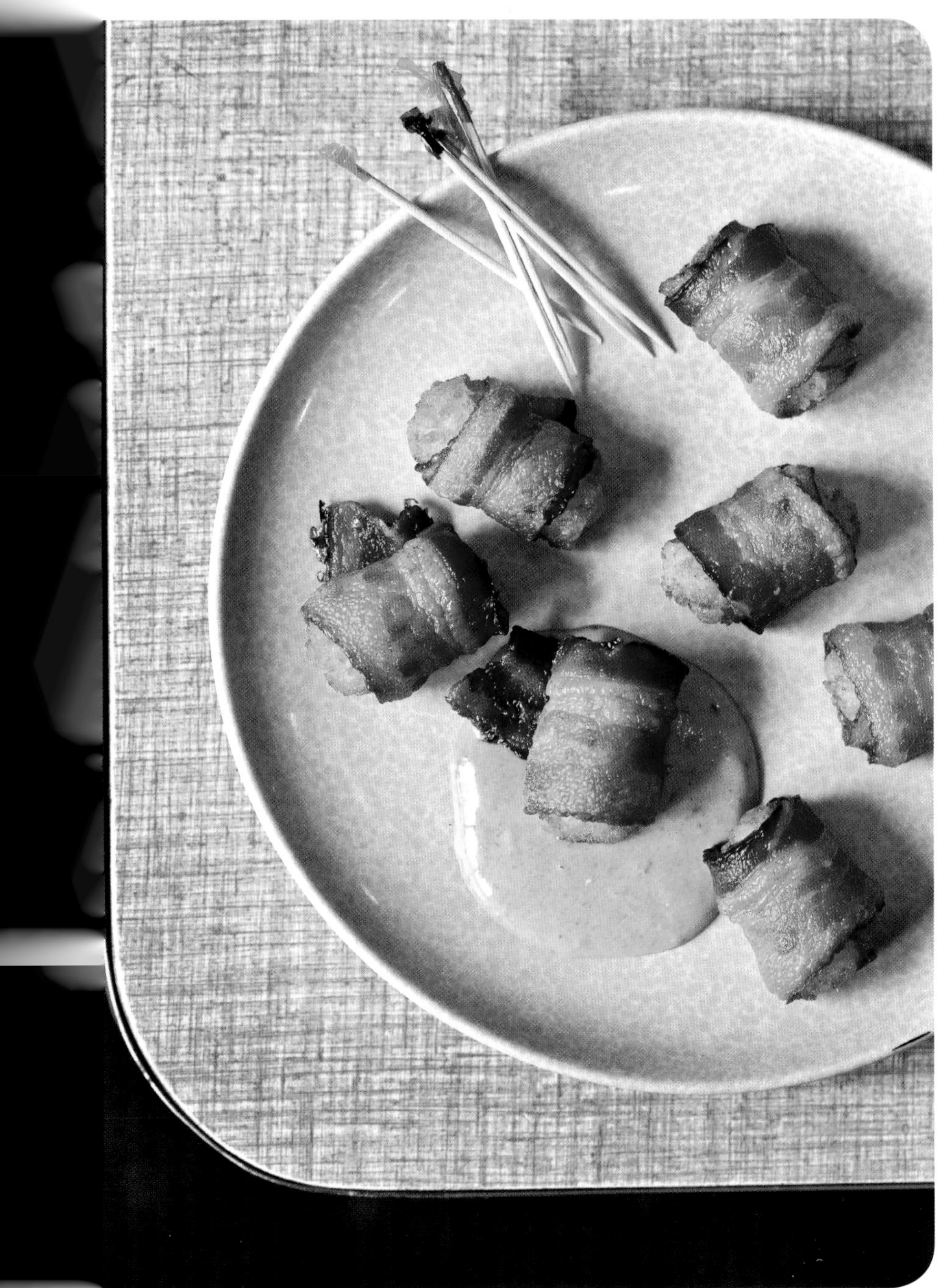

TOASTER PIZZA TOTS

As a kid one of my favorite things to do when I got home from school was to put pizza toppings on an English muffin and heat it in the toaster oven. I thought it might be fun to try this with a tot and it was a perfect swap! Just make sure you toast up the tot before you start so it stays crispy and holds together. *SERVES 1*

1 FROZEN MONSTER TOT
(AKA HASH BROWN PATTY)

1 TABLESPOON PIZZA SAUCE

2 TABLESPOONS SHREDDED
MOZZARELLA CHEESE

7 PEPPERONI SLICES
(OR TO TASTE)

DRIED OREGANO AND CRUSHED
RED PEPPER FLAKES,
FOR GARNISH (OPTIONAL)

1 Set the toaster oven to 400°F and line the tray with aluminum foil. Put the tot on the tray and cook to brown on both sides, about 10 minutes.

(Depending on your toaster oven, you might need to flip it or leave it in for multiple rounds. It is important to get it really crispy before topping it.)

2 Remove the tot from the toaster. Top with the sauce, then the cheese, and then the pepperoni.

3 Return the tot to the toaster and toast again until the cheese has melted and is starting to brown. Sprinkle with oregano and red pepper flakes to taste. Serve hot.

TOTKES with CAVIAR AND SOUR CREAM

Did you know you can make mini potato pancakes, or latkes, with store-bought tots? They aren't the most authentic version of the Jewish classic, but they are a great, easy way to satisfy a craving! I like to serve these with sour cream and applesauce, or—for a fancy occasion—some caviar with sour cream and chives, but feel free to get creative with your toppings (and check out the box on page 47 for other ideas). This recipe is easy to scale up for a crowd—simply turn more tots into totkes! *SERVES 2 OR 3*

10 FROZEN TOTS, DEFROSTED
(SEE BOX, PAGE 6)

VEGETABLE OR PEANUT OIL,
FOR FRYING

SOUR CREAM, FOR SERVING

CAVIAR OR APPLESAUCE,
FOR SERVING

CHOPPED OR SLICED FRESH CHIVES,
FOR GARNISH (OPTIONAL)

1 Heat 2 tablespoons of oil in a large, nonstick frying pan over medium-high heat. Add the tots (in batches if necessary, adding extra oil as needed) so they have a good 3 inches of space between them. Using a spatula, flatten the tots, pressing down on them one by one to form 2-inch-wide disks.

2 Cook the totkes, flipping once, until browned on both sides, about 3 minutes per side.

3 Transfer the cooked totkes to a paper towel to absorb excess grease, then transfer them to a plate. Top each tot with a dollop of sour cream and caviar and some chives, or with sour cream and applesauce. Serve immediately.

OTHER TOT CANAPÉS

Try one—or all—of these toppings for your totkes and coin-shape tot canapés!

• Horseradish Sauce (page 19), roasted red pepper, and a slice of medium-rare skirt steak (or rare roast beef)

• A slice of cherry tomato, one little basil leaf, and a mozzarella pearl

• Goat cheese, a slice of roasted peach, and a piece of crispy bacon

• A piece of cooked bacon, a slice of pineapple, and a pickled jalapeño

• Fresh guacamole and a sprinkling of pomegranate seeds

• A slice of Brie, a dollop of fancy jam, and a few almond slivers

• Cream cheese, a piece of smoked salmon, and fresh dill

• A cube of cantaloupe wrapped in prosciutto

• A slice of salami, a piece of Manchego, and a baby arugula leaf

• A slice of mango topped with crushed red pepper flakes and a small cooked shrimp

• Mayo, kernels of roasted corn, cotija cheese, and fresh cilantro

• Hummus, a cucumber slice, and a pitted olive

TOTAPEÑO POPPERS

Jalapeño poppers are a lot more versatile than most people think. You can fill these little pepper boats with so many different things! Here I opt for the traditional cream cheese filling with an added twist of tots and bacon. I like this recipe because you can still see the tots after they're nestled into their jalapeño boats and tucked in with a nice bacon blanket. *MAKES 16 POPPERS*

8 JALAPEÑO PEPPERS

1 BLOCK (8 OUNCES) CREAM CHEESE, AT ROOM TEMPERATURE

32 FROZEN TOTS

8 BACON STRIPS, HALVED CROSSWISE (TO MAKE 16 STRIPS)

1 Preheat the oven to 350°F.

2 Halve the jalapeños lengthwise, trying to keep the stem intact on both halves (this is easier to do if you start slicing at the stem end). Remove and discard the seeds and ribs.

3 Spread about a tablespoon of cream cheese into each jalapeño half. Place 2 tots, end to end, on top of the cream cheese.

4 Wrap a bacon strip around the center of each jalapeño half, aligning the strip so that the center covers the space where the tots meet, and wraps around to touch at the bottom of the jalapeño.

5 Place the jalapeños, filling-side up, on a wire rack set over a rimmed baking sheet and bake until the bacon is cooked through and the jalapeños are tender, about 20 minutes. Serve immediately.

SPINACH-TOT DIP

*T*ots replace artichoke in this '90s mainstay dip. It's creamy and indulgent, the perfect snack to have out next time your friends come over. I like serving it with pita chips because they are nice and sturdy and easily scoop up this thick dip. *SERVES 8*

I PACKAGE (10 OUNCES) CHOPPED FROZEN SPINACH, THAWED IN A SIEVE

I BLOCK (8 OUNCES) CREAM CHEESE, AT ROOM TEMPERATURE

¼ CUP MAYONNAISE

¼ CUP SOUR CREAM

I TABLESPOON FRESH LEMON JUICE

I TEASPOON HOT SAUCE

25 FROZEN TOTS, DEFROSTED (SEE BOX, PAGE 6)

½ CUP FRESHLY GRATED PARMESAN CHEESE

½ CUP (2 OUNCES) SHREDDED MOZZARELLA CHEESE

I GARLIC CLOVE, GRATED

KOSHER SALT AND FRESHLY GROUND BLACK PEPPER

1 Preheat the oven to 400°F.

2 Wrap the thawed spinach in a clean kitchen towel, cheesecloth, or paper towels and squeeze out all the excess liquid. Set aside.

3 Stir together the cream cheese, mayo, sour cream, lemon juice, and hot sauce in a large bowl until combined. Stir in the spinach, tots, cheeses, and garlic until combined and the tots are broken up a bit. Add salt and pepper to taste.

4 Transfer the dip to an 8-inch square baking dish and bake until heated through and browned and bubbly on top, about 25 minutes. Serve hot.

TOTS AND BRATS

I wanted to try cooking tots on the grill so I tested out a few different methods, but each time I struggled to keep the tots intact while they went from being frozen to fully cooked. Tots tend to fall apart when thawed, so the grill—with its live fire and open slats—is a danger zone. After a bunch of attempts, I discovered that sandwiching the tots between sausage slices kept them secure on a skewer, and was the perfect way for a tot to survive the grill. Note that you'll need four skewers for this recipe; if you're using wooden ones, soak them in water for 15 minutes to prevent them from burning.

MAKES 4 TOT KABOBS

2 BRATWURST SAUSAGES
(ABOUT 4 OUNCES EACH)

20 FROZEN COIN-SHAPE TOTS

VEGETABLE OIL, FOR GRILLING

SPICY CHEESE SAUCE (PAGE 16)
OR CHIPOTLE MAYO (PAGE 16),
FOR SERVING (I STRONGLY
RECOMMEND THE CHEESE
SAUCE HERE)

1 Slice the sausages crosswise into rounds that are slightly thinner than the tots.

2 Preheat the grill to medium heat.

3 Thread the sausage rounds and the tots onto each skewer, starting with a piece of sausage, then adding a tot, and alternating until there are 5 tots and 6 sausage rounds on each

skewer, with a sausage round on each end. Pack the pieces tightly so they stay together on the grill.

4 Brush the kabobs lightly with oil, then place them on the grill. Cook, turning occasionally and adjusting the heat as needed, until the kabobs are browned on all sides and heated through, 15 to 20 minutes.

5 Serve immediately with the dipping sauce of your choice.

TOT-CO SPRING ROLLS

What's a tot-co spring roll? A spring roll stuffed with taco-flavored tot filling, *obviously*. I like to use spring roll wrappers when I make apps like this for a party because they get super crispy and don't feel greasy or soggy as eggroll wrappers often do. I went with a taco flavor profile for these, but you can easily switch up the spices and fillings as long as the volume of fillings stays the same. *MAKES 15 SPRING ROLLS*

½ POUND GROUND BEEF

KOSHER SALT

1 SMALL ONION, DICED

3 JALAPEÑOS, STEMMED, SEEDED IF YOU WISH TO REDUCE THE HEAT, AND DICED

2 GARLIC CLOVES, MINCED

1 TABLESPOON GROUND CUMIN

1 TEASPOON SMOKED PAPRIKA

1 TEASPOON DRIED OREGANO

1 CHIPOTLE PEPPER IN ADOBO SAUCE, DICED

1 TABLESPOON HONEY

2 TABLESPOONS RED WINE VINEGAR

25 FROZEN TOTS, DEFROSTED (SEE BOX, PAGE 6)

1 BLOCK (8 OUNCES) CHEDDAR CHEESE, SHREDDED

¼ CUP CHOPPED FRESH CILANTRO LEAVES

15 SPRING ROLL WRAPPERS, DEFROSTED

VEGETABLE OR PEANUT OIL, FOR BAKING

1 Place the beef in a large frying pan over high heat. Lightly salt the beef and cook, stirring occasionally to break it up, until brown, about 10 minutes. Transfer the beef to a plate, leaving behind any fat in the pan.

2 Add the onion and jalapeños to the pan, turn the heat down to medium, and cook, stirring occasionally, until softened, about 10 minutes. Add the garlic and cook, stirring, until fragrant and lightly golden, about 2 minutes.

3 Return the beef to the pan. Add the cumin, paprika, oregano, chipotle pepper, honey, and vinegar and stir well to combine. Add 1 cup of water and bring to a simmer. Cook, stirring often, until the water has evaporated and the beef mixture is thick, about 20 minutes. Set aside and let cool completely.

4 Stir the tots into the cooled beef mixture, breaking up the tots as you stir. Stir in the cheese and cilantro until combined.

5 Working one at a time, lay each spring roll wrapper on a work surface and place about ¼ cup of the filling in the center. Roll it tightly, first tucking the sides of the wrapper up over the filling and then folding up the edge of the wrapper closest to you, to form a little roll. Use a little water on your fingertip to seal the seam. Repeat with the remaining wrappers and filling.

6 Brush each roll evenly with vegetable oil and place on a rimmed baking sheet. Bake, flipping occasionally to brown on all sides, about 20 minutes. Serve immediately.

Pot-Stuffed Pork Meatballs with Spicy Romesco Sauce

TOT-STUFFED PORK MEATBALLS *with* SPICY ROMESCO SAUCE

In hindsight, stuffing a meatball with a tot seems like an obvious idea, but I couldn't find any evidence of it being done before! After testing the merits of precooking the tots to add an extra dimension of brown flavor and crispness, my tasters unanimously agreed that the uncooked tots worked better. This is because browning the tots essentially seals them inside a crust, keeping them separate from the meat surrounding them. But when you wrap the thawed tots in meat, they really become one with the meatballs and the delicious pork flavor permeates the tots. *MAKES ABOUT 30 MEATBALLS; SERVES 8 TO 10*

FOR THE ROMESCO SAUCE

1 LARGE RED BELL PEPPER

1 HABAÑERO PEPPER, STEMMED, SEEDED, AND CHOPPED

25 ROASTED ALMONDS

2 GARLIC CLOVES

¼ CUP RED WINE VINEGAR

2 TABLESPOONS OLIVE OIL

KOSHER SALT AND FRESHLY GROUND BLACK PEPPER

CRUSHED RED PEPPER FLAKES

1 POUND GROUND PORK

KOSHER SALT AND FRESHLY
   GROUND BLACK PEPPER

½ CUP PLAIN BREADCRUMBS

2 TABLESPOONS MILK

1 GARLIC CLOVE, GRATED

1 CUP FRESHLY GRATED MANCHEGO
   CHEESE

¼ CUP CHOPPED FRESH ITALIAN
   (FLAT-LEAF) PARSLEY

1 LARGE EGG

ABOUT 30 FROZEN TOTS,
   DEFROSTED (SEE BOX, PAGE 6)

1 Preheat the broiler to high. Line a rimmed baking sheet with aluminum foil.

2 Make the romesco sauce: Put the bell pepper on the prepared baking sheet and broil, frequently rotating the pepper with tongs to blacken the skin evenly on all sides, about 5 minutes. Turn off the oven.

3 Transfer the charred pepper to a bowl, cover it with plastic wrap, and let it rest for 15 minutes.

4 Remove the charred pepper from the bowl and use your fingers to peel and discard its skin. Stem and seed the pepper and place the flesh in the bowl of a food processor. Add the habañero, almonds, garlic, vinegar, and olive oil. Add salt, black pepper, and red pepper flakes as desired, and process until smooth. Taste and adjust the seasonings as needed.

5 Make the meatballs: Put the ground pork in a bowl and season with ½ teaspoon each of salt and pepper. Add the breadcrumbs, milk, garlic, cheese, parsley, and egg and mix well to combine.

6 Preheat the broiler to high.

7 Meanwhile, form the meatballs one by one: Scoop 2 to 3 tablespoons of the pork mixture into your hand, place a tot in the center, and wrap the meat around the tot. The meatball shouldn't be huge—about golf ball size (you'll want a fairly thin layer of meat around the tot). Roll the meatball around between your palms to help round it and to seal the meat around the tot.

Place the finished meatballs on a rimmed baking sheet, making sure they don't touch.

8 Broil the meatballs, a few inches from the heat, until browned on top, 7 to 10 minutes, then flip them with a spatula and brown on the other side, about 7 minutes more. (Keep your eyes on them while they cook to make sure they don't burn.)

9 To serve, pile up the meatballs on a platter, place the romesco in a bowl, and pass toothpicks for dipping the meatballs into the sauce.

TOT-ROGI

Pierogi ruskie—the kind filled with potato and cheese—is not the most popular pierogi in Poland, but it definitely is here in the United States. In fact, it's the kind that most Americans know simply as pierogi. Using tots in place of the typical mashed potato filling adds an unexpected texture to this classic dish. *MAKES 15 TOT-ROGI*

3 CUPS ALL-PURPOSE FLOUR

1 LARGE EGG

4 TABLESPOONS (½ STICK) UNSALTED BUTTER, MELTED

½ CUP SOUR CREAM, PLUS EXTRA FOR SERVING

2 TABLESPOONS (¼ STICK) UNSALTED BUTTER, AT ROOM TEMPERATURE

1 LARGE ONION, DICED

30 FROZEN TOTS

1 BLOCK (8 OUNCES) CHEDDAR CHEESE, SHREDDED

CHOPPED FRESH CHIVES, FOR GARNISH

1 Combine the flour, egg, melted butter, and ½ cup of the sour cream in a large bowl and mix with a wooden spoon until combined and a dough forms. When the dough becomes too stiff to stir with the spoon, use your hands to knead it in the bowl until it is smooth, about 5 minutes. Remove the dough from the bowl and wrap it in plastic wrap. Let it rest in the fridge while you mix the filling (it will keep, wrapped and refrigerated, for up to 2 days).

2 Melt 1 tablespoon of the room-temperature butter in a large frying pan over medium heat. Add the onion and cook, stirring often, until caramelized, about 25 minutes. Set aside.

3 Place the tots in a large, microwave-safe bowl and microwave on high for 3 minutes, pausing once to stir gently.

4 Mix the caramelized onions and the shredded cheese into the tots and stir well, breaking up the tots and combining everything. Set aside.

5 Bring a large pot of water to a boil over high heat.

6 Meanwhile, lightly flour a work surface. Remove the pierogi dough from the fridge and place it on the work surface. Using a rolling pin, roll it out into a sheet about ⅛ inch thick. Using a 3½-inch cookie cutter or a pint glass (that's what I usually use!), cut out about 15 rounds of the dough (feel free to reroll the scraps to get a couple more).

7 Put a heaping tablespoon of filling in the center of each dough round. Fold the dough over itself into a half-moon shape, and use the tines of a fork to seal the edge.

8 Add the pierogi to the boiling water and cook until they begin to float, about 5 minutes. Using a slotted spoon, transfer the cooked pierogi to a cooling rack to dry.

9 Melt the remaining 1 tablespoon of butter in a large frying pan over medium-high heat and, working in batches to avoid crowding the pan, add the boiled pierogi and fry until browned on both sides, about 5 minutes per side.

10 Serve hot, sprinkled with the chives.

CHEESY TOT SKINS

The best part of potato skins is the crispy, salty crunch of the skin itself. Well, that and bacon. But sometimes it's hard to get the skins crispy in your own kitchen. Once again, tots are here to save the day. Press the tots into a mini muffin tin to form crispy cups perfect for any filling you could imagine.

MAKES 24 TOT SKINS; SERVES 10

VEGETABLE OR PEANUT OIL, FOR GREASING THE MUFFIN TIN

2 POUNDS FROZEN TOTS (ABOUT 90 TOTS), DEFROSTED (SEE BOX, PAGE 5)

1 LARGE EGG

1 POUND BACON, COOKED AND CRUMBLED

2 CUPS (8 OUNCES) SHREDDED CHEDDAR CHEESE

1 CUP SOUR CREAM

½ CUP CHOPPED FRESH CHIVES

1 Preheat the oven to 450°F. Grease the wells of a mini muffin tin with oil and set aside.

2 Place the tots in a large bowl and, using a potato masher or fork, mash them until they are a uniform consistency. Add the egg and stir until incorporated.

3 Scoop 2 tablespoons of the tot mixture into each well of the mini muffin tin, and use your thumb to press the tot mixture into a cup shape. The tot mixture should be about ¼ inch thick.

4 Bake until the tot cups are crispy, about 15 minutes.

5 Remove the tin from the oven and top each tot cup with some of the crumbled bacon and some of the cheese. Bake until the cheese has melted, another 5 minutes.

6 Remove the tin from the oven and let cool for 1 to 2 minutes, then pop the cups out onto a cooling rack. Top each tot skin with sour cream and chives, transfer to a platter, and serve warm.

TOT-STUFFED MUSHROOMS

Stuffed mushrooms may sound like an old-fashioned appetizer, but they are always delicious and when you play around with the fillings, you can make the flavors much more modern. This version uses a filling of mashed-up tots combined with Italian sausage, bell pepper and onion, and creamy mozzarella cheese. While the mushrooms bake, the stuffing gets nice and brown, really amping up that tot texture. *MAKES 25 STUFFED MUSHROOMS; SERVES 5 OR 6*

1 HOT ITALIAN SAUSAGE
   (ABOUT 4 OUNCES),
   CASING REMOVED

1 SMALL ONION, DICED

1 RED BELL PEPPER, STEMMED,
   SEEDED, AND DICED

1 POUND FROZEN TOTS
   (ABOUT 45 TOTS)

25 BABY BELLA MUSHROOMS
   (ABOUT 1 POUND)

2 CUPS (8 OUNCES) SHREDDED
   MOZZARELLA CHEESE

1 Place the sausage in a large frying pan over medium-high heat and cook, breaking up the sausage into small pieces with a wooden spoon, until browned, about 5 minutes.

2 Add the onion and bell pepper and cook, stirring often and scraping the bottom of the pan, until the vegetables have softened, about 10 minutes. Add the tots and stir well to incorporate. Turn the heat down to low and cook until the tots have defrosted and break apart when you press on them, about 5 minutes. Set aside.

3 Preheat the oven to 400°F. Line a rimmed baking sheet with parchment paper and set aside.

4 Meanwhile, remove the mushroom stems and gills, rinse the mushrooms lightly, and pat them dry.

5 Pour the tots mixture into a large bowl and add the cheese, stirring well to combine and breaking up all the tots.

6 One by one, stuff the cavity of each mushroom with a few tablespoons of the tot mixture (depending on the size of the mushroom). The mushrooms should be overstuffed and tightly packed so it looks like a tower of filling coming out of each. Place the mushrooms, stuffed-side up, on the prepared baking sheet.

7 Bake until the mushrooms are cooked through and the tot mixture is crispy on top, about 20 minutes. (If they aren't crisping up, finish them under the broiler on high heat.) Serve hot.

TOTZARELLA STICKS

My first thought with this recipe was to make a corn dog with tots for the breading. But once I had that idea, the inspiration started spiraling in every direction. What else could I bread with tots and deep-fry? My favorites were mozzarella sticks and hot dogs (which I like to serve on sticks for a corn dog effect—see variation), but you'll find a bunch of other ideas in the box on page 66. *MAKES 12 STICKS*

VEGETABLE OR PEANUT OIL,
  FOR FRYING

1 CUP ALL-PURPOSE FLOUR

3 LARGE EGGS

2 POUNDS FROZEN TOTS (ABOUT
  90 TOTS; SEE NOTE)

6 STRING CHEESE STICKS,
  CUT IN HALF CROSSWISE
  TO MAKE 12 PIECES

1 Pour oil to a depth of 4 inches into a large, heavy-bottomed pot. Heat the oil over medium-high heat until a deep-fry or candy thermometer inserted into the oil reaches 375°F.

2 Place the flour on a plate. In a small bowl, whisk together 2 of the eggs; set this egg wash beside the plate.

3 Place the tots in a large microwave-safe bowl and microwave on high at 1-minute intervals, stirring after each, until defrosted and broken down, about 5 minutes total. Add the remaining egg and stir until combined. Place this tot mixture next to the egg wash.

4 Dip a cheese stick into the flour to coat, then dip it into the egg wash. Scoop up a handful of the tot mixture, flatten it in the palm of your hand, and put the coated cheese stick in the middle. Form the tot mixture around the cheese stick, making a thin, even layer that covers the cheese stick completely. Set on a plate. Repeat with the remaining cheese sticks and tot mixture.

5 Fry the coated cheese sticks in two batches until golden brown and crispy (keep an eye on them—you want to pull them from the oil just before any filling leaks out), about 3 minutes. Serve hot.

NOTE: If you'd like to make the tot breading from scratch, feel free to use the Homemade Tots mixture on page 9 (before you form it into tots!) in place of the frozen tots.

VARIATION:

To make tot-dogs, simply use hot dogs in place of the string cheese. I like to serve a combination of tot-dogs and totzarella sticks.

OTHER THINGS YOU CAN COAT IN TOTS AND DEEP-FRY

Because WHY NOT? Use the tot mixture and breading technique on page 65 as a guide, and let your imagination run wild. (One note of caution: Unfortunately Brussels sprouts and onion rings don't work. I've tried.)

CHICKEN: This takes fried chicken to a whole new place. Use chicken tenders and fry until cooked through, about 5 minutes.

FISH: It's like fish and chips but ALL IN ONE. This works best with cod loins.

SHRIMP: Keep the tails sticking out so you have a handle. Fry until lightly browned.

PICKLE SPEARS: Fry until golden (skip pickle chips here—they won't work).

MAC AND CHEESE: Make it, chill it, cut it, bread it, fry it until golden.

RISOTTO: Arancini with a twist! Form risotto into small balls, chill them, bread them, fry them until lightly browned.

GREEN TOMATOES: The juicy, sour tomato will be exploding with flavor. Make the tomato slices thick and fry them until crispy.

ZUCCHINI: Again, keep it in spears and not circles.

CHEESEBURGER TOT SLIDERS

Why have a burger with some tots on the side when you can just build a burger with tots as the bun! These mini tot sliders are first and foremost insanely cute. Believe it or not, they are actually pretty easy to make, too. But most important—they are extremely delicious. If you serve your friends these sliders when they come over for the big game, they will lose their minds! *MAKES 16 MINI SLIDERS*

32 FROZEN COIN-SHAPE TOTS

2 TABLESPOONS VEGETABLE OR PEANUT OIL

½ POUND 85% LEAN GROUND BEEF

KOSHER SALT AND FRESHLY GROUND BLACK PEPPER

4 SLICES AMERICAN CHEESE

KETCHUP, FOR TOPPING

MUSTARD, FOR TOPPING

16 GHERKINS

1 Preheat the oven to 450°F.

2 Place the tots on a rimmed baking sheet and drizzle them with the oil. Toss the tots gently to coat evenly with the oil, then spread them out in an even layer. Bake, undisturbed, until they are browned on the bottom, about 15 minutes. Flip the tots with a spatula and bake until they are browned and crisp on top, about 10 minutes.

3 Meanwhile, form and cook the burgers: Line a clean work surface with a sheet of wax paper and put the ground beef on top. Put another sheet of wax paper on top of the beef and press it down into a 4- by 6-inch rectangle. Remove the top piece of wax paper and season the meat with salt and pepper to taste. Cut the meat into sixteen 1- by 1½-inch rectangles.

4 Break each slice of cheese into quarters, and fold each quarter over to make 16 pieces of double-thick cheese. Set aside.

5 Cook the burgers in a large nonstick frying pan over high heat, until browned on one side, about 5 minutes. Flip the burgers, lay a piece of double-thick cheese on each, and cook until the burgers are cooked through and the cheese has melted, about 5 minutes more. (You may have to do this in two batches if you don't have a big enough pan.)

6 Remove the tot "buns" from the oven and top half with the cooked cheeseburger patties. Squeeze a tiny bit of ketchup and mustard onto each cheeseburger, then top with the gherkin. Finally, poke a food pick through the center of each of the remaining tot buns. Place one on top of a cheeseburger stack and stab the food pick all the way down through the center to make a sandwich. Repeat with the remaining tot buns, toppings, and cheeseburgers.

7 Serve hot. If not serving immediately, reheat them on a baking sheet in the oven at 200°F for 5 minutes.

DEVILED TOTS

When I started experimenting with deviled tots, I was making deviled eggs with tots as the filling, and they were a big failure. I almost gave up on the idea! Finally I realized deviled tots should be all potato (just like deviled eggs are all eggs), and this recipe really took off. These look super fancy and would be great at a party as passed hors d'oeuvres. This recipe uses coin-shape tots (sometimes sold as Crispy Crowns!), which are an awesome vehicle for other toppings (see box, page 47).

MAKES 25 DEVILED TOTS; SERVES 5 OR 6

1 TABLESPOON VEGETABLE OIL, FOR GREASING THE BAKING SHEET

25 FROZEN COIN-SHAPE TOTS

1 CUP MASHED OR RICED COOKED POTATO (ABOUT 1 LARGE PEELED, COOKED RUSSET POTATO)

¼ CUP MAYONNAISE

2 TABLESPOONS YELLOW MUSTARD

1 TABLESPOON APPLE CIDER VINEGAR

1 TEASPOON HOT SAUCE

½ TEASPOON SWEET PAPRIKA, PLUS EXTRA FOR GARNISH

1 TABLESPOON CHOPPED FRESH CHIVES, FOR GARNISH

1 Preheat the oven to 450°F. Lightly oil a rimmed baking sheet.

2 Spread the tots out on the prepared baking sheet in an even layer. Bake, carefully flipping the tots halfway through, until they are browned evenly, about 20 minutes.

3 Meanwhile, place the mashed potatoes, mayonnaise, mustard, vinegar, hot sauce, and the ½ teaspoon paprika in a large bowl and stir until combined and smooth. Load the mixture into a piping bag (or put it in a zip-top bag and cut off a small corner).

4 Transfer the tots to a serving platter and pipe the potato mixture onto the tots, one by one, in a decorative fashion.

5 Top the deviled tots with the chives and a sprinkling of paprika and serve immediately.

CHAPTER 3

TOT O' THE MORNING TO YOU

TOTS AT THE BREAKFAST TABLE

BREAKFAST BUR-TOT-O

Breakfast burritos often have potatoes in them, unlike their rest-of-the-day counterparts. But the taters usually end up getting mushy and kind of disappearing into the burrito, becoming more of a dense filler than a surprising highlight. Tots to the rescue once again! Here they save our breakfast burrito from mundane soggy potatoes and elevate it to a cheesy, eggy, crunch-inflected bur-tot-o. *MAKES 2 BURRITOS*

VEGETABLE OR PEANUT OIL, FOR FRYING

4 OUNCES LOOSE MEXICAN CHORIZO (SEE NOTE)

12 FROZEN TOTS

4 LARGE EGGS

2 LARGE (10-INCH) FLOUR TORTILLAS

¼ CUP SHREDDED CHEDDAR CHEESE

1 LARGE AVOCADO, PITTED, PEELED, AND THINLY SLICED (OPTIONAL)

½ CUP PICO DE GALLO (PAGE 23)

1 Heat 1 tablespoon of the oil in a large frying pan over medium-high heat. Add the chorizo and cook, stirring occasionally, until browned, about 5 minutes. Remove the chorizo from the pan with a slotted spoon, leaving the fat behind.

2 Add the tots to the fat and cook over medium-high heat, turning occasionally, until browned and crisp on all sides, about 3 minutes per side. Remove from the pan and let drain on paper towels.

3 There should still be enough fat in the pan to cook the eggs, but if not, add a little more oil to coat the pan. Crack the eggs, one by one, into the pan and cook over medium heat, flipping once during cooking, until the whites are set but the yolks are still runny, about 3 minutes.

4 Meanwhile, place each tortilla on a microwave-safe plate and divide the cheese between them. One at a time, microwave each tortilla on high heat to soften the tortilla and melt the cheese slightly, about 30 seconds.

5 Build each burrito in a warm tortilla, beginning with slices of the avocado (if using), then 6 of the tots, followed by half of the cooked chorizo, 2 of the eggs, and half of the pico. Roll your burritos in the classic burrito shape by folding one edge over the filling, then folding up and tucking in the sides, and then rolling it into a tight cylinder. Wrap with aluminum foil to help retain the shape and give it that traditional burrito-shop feel.

6 Serve immediately.

NOTE: Mexican chorizo is an uncooked sausage mixture that's typically sold loose (unlike Spanish chorizo, which is stuffed into a casing and dried). You can find it with the other raw meats at a supermarket.

TOTS BENEDICT

For a long time Eggs Benedict was my number one go-to when I was out for breakfast or brunch, mainly because I was too intimidated to make poached eggs and hollandaise at home. Turns out, though, that neither one is as hard to prepare as it seems, and once you start making them at home they become second nature. I love stacking these tot "Bennies" really high so the hollandaise and egg yolks drip beautifully down the tower of tots. *SERVES 2*

32 FROZEN TOTS

1 TABLESPOON VEGETABLE OR PEANUT OIL

4 CANADIAN BACON OR HAM SLICES

3 LARGE EGG YOLKS PLUS 4 WHOLE LARGE EGGS (THE FRESHER THE BETTER)

1 TABLESPOON FRESH LEMON JUICE

PINCH OF KOSHER SALT

½ CUP (1 STICK) UNSALTED BUTTER, MELTED

1 TABLESPOON SRIRACHA, PLUS EXTRA FOR SERVING (OPTIONAL)

2 ENGLISH MUFFINS

1 Preheat the oven to 450°F.

2 Place the tots on a rimmed baking sheet and drizzle them with the oil. Toss the tots to coat evenly with the oil, then spread them out in an even layer. Bake until browned on the bottom, about 10 minutes.

3 Flip the tots with a spatula, scoot them to one side of the baking sheet, and add the Canadian bacon to the other side. Continue baking until the tots are browned all over, about 10 minutes more. Remove from the oven and transfer to a paper towel to drain.

4 Make the hollandaise sauce: In a large metal or glass bowl, whisk the 3 egg yolks with the lemon juice and salt until they have increased in volume and lightened, about 3 minutes.

5 Assemble a makeshift double boiler: Fill a medium-size pot halfway with water and place over medium heat until the water steams; lower the heat if it starts to simmer. Put the bowl with the egg mixture on the steaming pot, making sure the bottom does not touch the water, and heat the mixture, whisking constantly, until it triples in volume and the whisk leaves a trail in the bowl as you stir. It will read 145°F degrees on an instant-read thermometer. (To prevent the mixture from overheating, put the bowl over the steam for 15 seconds, then take it off for another 15 seconds, whisking the whole time.)

6 Drizzle in ½ teaspoon of the melted butter, whisking to fully incorporate. Continue adding the melted butter in small increments, and then larger increments, whisking constantly, until the butter is incorporated and the sauce is nice and thick. Whisk in the sriracha (if using).

Cover the bowl and turn off the heat, resting the bowl atop the double boiler to keep warm.

7 Poach the 4 whole eggs: Fill a medium-size saucepan three-quarters full with water and bring to a boil over high heat, then lower to a simmer. Crack an egg into a mesh strainer, shaking out and discarding the loose egg whites, leaving only the firmer portion of the egg white that surrounds the yolk. Gently lower the strainer into the simmering water and tip the egg into it. Repeat with a second egg. Let the eggs cook until the whites are set and the yolks are still runny, about 4 minutes. Remove the eggs from the water with a slotted spoon and transfer to a plate. Repeat with the remaining eggs, making sure the water is simmering before adding them.

8 While the eggs cook, split and toast the English muffins.

9 Build the Bennies: Divide the English muffin halves among two plates, top each with a slice of the Canadian bacon and 8 tots. Next, top each stack with a poached egg, and then drown it in hollandaise sauce. Serve immediately, with more sriracha if you like.

TOT MIGAS

Migas is the perfect I'm-hungover-let's-throw-everything-into-a pan-with-eggs type of meal. It's got tortillas, salsa, eggs, and cheese, so tossing some crispy tots into the mix seemed like a no-brainer to me. Each bite is like eating eggy nacho hangover medicine.

SERVES 4

1 CUP PICO DE GALLO
    (PAGE 23)

VEGETABLE OR PEANUT OIL,
    FOR FRYING

4 SMALL (6-INCH) SOFT CORN
    TORTILLAS, TORN INTO BITE-
    SIZE PIECES

20 FROZEN TOTS

9 LARGE EGGS

KOSHER SALT AND FRESHLY
    GROUND BLACK PEPPER

½ CUP SHREDDED CHEDDAR CHEESE

HOT SAUCE, FOR SERVING

1 Place the pico in a mesh strainer set over a bowl (or in the sink) to drain any excess liquid, about 15 minutes. (Excess liquid in the scrambled eggs will give them a runny texture.)

2 Meanwhile, heat 2 tablespoons of the oil in a large, nonstick frying pan over high heat. Working in two batches (and adding a bit more oil as needed), add the tortilla pieces and fry, turning occasionally, until golden brown and crispy, about 3 minutes. Remove from the heat and place on paper towels to drain. Reserve the pan.

3 The tots are up next. In the same pan, adding more oil as needed, fry the tots to brown on all sides, about 3 minutes per side. Don't mess with them too much—you don't want them to break apart. Remove from the heat and place the tots on a paper towel to drain. Reserve the pan and any oil in it.

4 Crack the eggs into a large bowl. Season with salt and pepper and beat together until the mixture is smooth. Place the pan over medium heat and add the eggs (add more oil if needed). When the eggs begin to set, add the cooked tortillas and tots and continue to cook, stirring gently, for 2 minutes. Add the cheese, stirring gently to incorporate, and cook until the cheese has melted and the eggs are almost fully set, 2 minutes more. Stir in the pico and remove from the heat.

5 Serve immediately with hot sauce on the side.

TOT CRUST QUICHE *with* BACON AND CARAMELIZED ONION

People have been skipping the pastry crust on a quiche for years and swapping it out for potatoes, but using tots actually makes the whole thing even easier and much crispier. You can customize this recipe endlessly by adding other fillings, but this version with bacon, caramelized onion, and a little arugula is my favorite. *SERVES 4*

1 POUND FROZEN TOTS (ABOUT 45 TOTS), DEFROSTED (SEE BOX, PAGE 6)

8 LARGE EGGS

NONSTICK COOKING SPRAY, FOR GREASING THE PAN

½ POUND BACON (ABOUT 10 STRIPS)

1 LARGE ONION, DICED

4 OUNCES ARUGULA

1 CUP MILK

1 CUP (4 OUNCES) SHREDDED PROVOLONE CHEESE

1 Preheat the oven to 400°F.

2 Mash up the tots in a large bowl, add 1 of the eggs, and stir to incorporate.

3 Lightly grease a 9-inch pie pan with cooking spray and press your tot mixture into it and up the sides to form a crust (try to make the crust even throughout).

4 Bake the crust until it is starting to brown on the

edges, about 20 minutes. Set the crust aside to cool (keep the oven on).

5 Chop the bacon crosswise into ½-inch pieces and cook in a large frying pan over medium heat, stirring occasionally, until crispy, about 7 minutes. Remove the bacon from the pan and allow it to drain on a paper towel. Drain the bacon fat from the pan, reserving about 2 tablespoons in the pan.

6 Heat the reserved bacon fat over low heat, add the onion, and cook until it is medium-brown, about 20 minutes. Stir in the arugula and cook until wilted. Remove from the heat.

7 In a large bowl, whisk together the 7 remaining eggs, the milk, and the cheese. Stir in the bacon mixture.

8 Set the pie pan on a rimmed baking sheet and pour the egg mixture into the crust, using a spoon to spread the fillings evenly. Bake until the filling is set and the center doesn't wobble, about 40 minutes.

9 Allow the quiche to cool for 5 minutes before serving.

Tot Crust Quiche will keep, in the pie pan covered in aluminum foil in the refrigerator, for 1 to 2 days. To reheat it, pop it in the oven at 350°F for 10 minutes.

TOT SHAKSHUKA

Shakshuka was on hardly anyone's radar in America a few years ago, but it has skyrocketed to become the hottest breakfast around, appearing on brunch menus across the country. I love the simplicity of the dish and the strong flavors that develop so quickly. Topping it with a handful of tots adds much needed crunch. *SERVES 3*

---

24 FROZEN TOTS

2 TABLESPOONS PLUS 1 TEASPOON VEGETABLE OR PEANUT OIL

½ POUND SAUSAGE, PREFERABLY LAMB MERGUEZ OR BREAKFAST SAUSAGE, CASING REMOVED

1 SMALL ONION, DICED

1 GREEN BELL PEPPER, STEMMED, SEEDED, AND DICED

1 GARLIC CLOVE, MINCED

1 TEASPOON GROUND CUMIN

1 TEASPOON SMOKED PAPRIKA

1 CAN (28 OUNCES) DICED TOMATOES WITH THEIR JUICES

6 LARGE EGGS

1 Preheat the oven to 450°F.

2 Place the tots on a rimmed baking sheet and drizzle them with 2 tablespoons of oil. Toss the tots gently to coat them evenly with the oil, then spread them out in an even layer. Bake, carefully flipping the tots halfway through, until they are browned evenly and crispy, about 20 minutes.

3 Meanwhile, heat 1 teaspoon of the oil in a large frying pan over high heat. Add the sausage and cook, stirring occasionally to break up the meat, until it is browned and cooked through, about 5 minutes.

4 Reduce the heat to medium-high. Add the onion and bell pepper and cook, stirring occasionally, until the vegetables have softened, about 10 minutes. Add the garlic, cumin, and paprika, stir to incorporate, and cook until the garlic is fragrant and lightly golden, about 2 minutes.

5 Stir in the tomatoes, reduce the heat to low, and simmer to allow the flavors to come together, 10 to 15 minutes.

6 Turn the oven temperature down to 350°F.

7 Divide the sauce among 3 shallow, 6-inch round individual baking dishes. Use a spoon to make 2 indentations in the sauce in each dish. Crack an egg into each indentation (two eggs per baking dish). Scatter 8 tots on top of each dish.

8 Bake until the egg whites are set but the yolks are still soft, about 15 minutes.

9 Let cool momentarily, then serve hot.

CHICKEN AND TOT-WAFFLES

Waffled tots offer two benefits in one: The tots get super crispy when pressed in a waffle iron, and of course they look really cool. The key to waffling tots is making sure they are at room temperature or warmer when they hit the waffle iron. A waffle iron is not very powerful, so it will lose its heat and take a long time to regain it if you try to waffle cold tots. Paired with nice buttermilk-marinated fried chicken and a sweet-and-spicy syrup, these tot waffles really shine. (Note that the chicken needs to marinate for at least two hours, so you may want to plan ahead.) *MAKES 8 CHICKEN PIECES AND 8 TO 10 WAFFLES; SERVES 4 HUNGRY PEOPLE*

FOR THE CHICKEN

8 CHICKEN TENDERS

1 CUP BUTTERMILK

1 TABLESPOON HOT SAUCE

2 GARLIC CLOVES, GRATED

KOSHER SALT AND FRESHLY
   GROUND BLACK PEPPER

VEGETABLE OR PEANUT OIL,
   FOR FRYING

2 CUPS ALL-PURPOSE FLOUR

1 TABLESPOON SMOKED PAPRIKA

3 LARGE EGGS

ABOUT 4 POUNDS FROZEN TOTS
(AMOUNT WILL VARY DEPENDING
ON THE SIZE OF YOUR WAFFLE
IRON)

BUTTER OR NONSTICK COOKING
SPRAY, FOR GREASING THE
WAFFLE IRON

$^3/_4$ CUP PURE MAPLE SYRUP

$^1/_3$ CUP KETCHUP

$^1/_4$ CUP HOT SAUCE

1. Place the chicken in a large bowl. Add the buttermilk, hot sauce, garlic, and ½ teaspoon each of salt and pepper and stir to combine and coat. Cover and marinate in the fridge for 2 hours or overnight.

2. Pour oil to a depth of 4 inches into a large, heavy-bottomed pot. Heat the oil over medium-high heat until a deep-fry or candy thermometer inserted into the oil reaches 375°F.

3. While the oil heats, set up the breading station: Combine the flour, paprika, and ½ teaspoon each of salt and pepper in a wide, shallow bowl. In a medium-size bowl, whisk together the eggs and season with salt and pepper; pour the eggs into another wide, shallow bowl and set it beside the flour mixture.

4. Remove a piece of chicken from the marinade, letting any excess marinade drip back into the bowl, and dredge it in the flour mixture. Shake off any excess, then dip the chicken into the egg wash to coat. Finally, dredge the chicken through the flour again to fully coat it, and place it on a clean plate. Repeat with the remaining chicken.

5. Preheat the oven to 170°F or the lowest temperature.

6. Working in two batches, fry the chicken in the oil until golden brown and crispy, about 8 minutes. Transfer the cooked chicken to a cooling rack (or paper towel–lined plate) to drain. Then keep warm on a baking sheet in the oven.

7. Make the waffles: Put half of the tots on a microwave-safe plate and microwave on high until defrosted (they should be room temperature or warmer), about 2 minutes. Repeat with the remaining tots. (The defrosted tots will be fragile, so handle them carefully.)

8 Preheat your waffle iron and grease it with butter or cooking spray.

9 Fill the bottom half of the waffle iron with tots. Really fill it—you want to pack in more tots than you think will fit because that helps them stick together and form one big waffle-tot. (I use about 25 tots per 5-inch waffle.)

10 Close the waffle iron and cook until the tots are melded and crispy on both sides, about 5 minutes. Place the cooked waffle on a plate and keep warm in the oven. Repeat with the remaining tots for a total of 8 to 10 waffles.

11 Make the spicy syrup: Stir together the maple syrup, ketchup, and hot sauce in a measuring cup.

12 Divide the tot-waffles among 4 plates, stacking them on top of each other, and top each stack with 2 chicken tenders. Pour the spicy syrup evenly over the chicken and waffles. Serve immediately.

SC-TOT-CH EGG

I featured a hash brown–wrapped egg a while back on my blog and to this day it is still one of the most popular recipes on the site. What makes it so good is soft-boiling the egg to keep the yolk runny when you cut into it. This version takes it one step further by adding a layer of sausage in between the crispy tot crust and the egg inside. *MAKES 4 EGGS*

6 LARGE EGGS

VEGETABLE OR PEANUT OIL, FOR FRYING

½ POUND LOOSE BREAKFAST SAUSAGE

½ CUP ALL-PURPOSE FLOUR

36 FROZEN TOTS

1 Fill a small pot with water to a depth of ½ inch and bring to a rapid boil over high heat. Add 4 whole eggs, cover, and let cook for 6 minutes and 30 seconds (use a timer!). Remove the pot from the heat and uncover. Run cold water into the pot and carefully pour out the hot water. Repeat 2 or 3 times until the pot and water remain cold. Let the eggs sit in the cold water for a few minutes until they are cool to the touch.

2 Remove the eggs from the water and carefully peel and dry them. Set aside on a plate.

3 Pour oil to a depth of 4 inches into a large, heavy-bottomed pot. Heat the oil over medium-high heat until a deep-fry or candy thermometer inserted into the oil reaches 375°F.

4 Meanwhile, divide and shape the sausage into 4 equal-size balls and set aside

on a plate. Set up your breading station: Put the flour on a plate, crack 1 egg into a small bowl and beat it with a fork, and set the bowl beside the plate.

5 Place the tots in a large microwave-safe bowl and microwave them on high at 1-minute intervals, stirring after each, until thawed and fully broken up, 4 to 5 minutes total. Beat the remaining egg in a small bowl and stir it into the tots to incorporate. Set the tots mixture next to the flour and beaten egg in the breading station; lay a sheet of wax paper beside it.

6 Gently coat a soft-boiled egg in flour and shake off any excess. Flatten one of the sausage balls in your hand and wrap it around the egg to cover

it completely. Next, coat the sausage layer in flour and shake off any excess. Dip the coated boiled egg in the beaten egg, shaking off any excess, and finally, scoop up about ½ cup of the tots mixture and form it around the egg to cover it completely with a thin layer. Place on the wax paper. Repeat with the remaining boiled eggs.

 7 Set a cooling rack over a layer of paper towels. Working in batches of two, carefully drop the Sc-tot-ch eggs into the hot oil and cook until browned on all sides, about 5 minutes. Transfer to the cooling rack to drain.

8 Serve hot.

TOAD IN A TOT HOLE

*T*oad in a hole (or egg in a hole) is many people's favorite breakfast. It conjures images of being a kid and having your mom or dad cook you a simple hot breakfast before school. It's this nostalgia that makes it a classic. Toad in a *tot* hole is a fun twist on the dish, evoking the original but with an unexpected tot update. *SERVES 1*

1 TO 2 TABLESPOONS UNSALTED
  BUTTER

1 FROZEN MONSTER TOT (AKA HASH
  BROWN PATTY)

1 LARGE EGG

KOSHER SALT AND FRESHLY
  GROUND BLACK PEPPER

HOT SAUCE (OPTIONAL)

1 Line a plate with a paper towel. Melt 1 tablespoon of the butter in a nonstick skillet over medium heat. Add the tot and cook, flipping halfway through, until golden on both sides, about 8 minutes. Remove from the pan and cool on the prepared plate.

2 Using a 2-inch round cookie cutter, biscuit cutter, juice glass, or sharp knife, cut a hole in the center of the hash brown. (It's best to cut two overlapping holes to form an oval shape.)

3 Add another tablespoon of butter to the pan if needed. Return the tot to the pan, crack the egg into the center, and season with salt and pepper. Cook until the egg has fully set on the bottom, about 3 minutes. Using a spatula, carefully and gently flip the egg-filled tot and cook until the whites are set and the yolk has thickened slightly but is still runny, about 3 minutes more.

4 Serve immediately, with hot sauce on the side, if you like.

An UNOFFICIAL and INCOMPLETE TIMELINE of the TATER TOT

1953: Tater tots are born. Ore-Ida's founders experiment with uses for the scraps created during french fry production, and hit on the winning combination of potato shavings, seasonings, and flour formed into savory morsels and deep-fried. Potato nugget nirvana attained!

1956: Ore-Ida's Tater Tots go on sale to the public, but people are not interested in the new product. Marketing professionals credit this to the fact that the tots are priced very low, owing to their scrap-heap origins.

1957: New packaging and pricing are introduced, and the tots begin their climb to fame.

1980s: A Cincinnati chili parlor offers topped tots on the menu—could this be a precursor to the topped-tot craze that follows decades later?

2004: Awkward screen teen Napoleon Dynamite asks the question that's on everyone's mind: "You gonna eat your tots?"

2009: February 2 is designated National Tater Tot Day.

2010: A proposed ban on potatoes in federal child nutrition programs spurs nationwide panic among schoolchildren, with one Washington State second-grader exclaiming, "That would be so not cool. I love Tater Tots."

2012: *Business Insider* issues a "nostalgic trend alert" stating "tater tots are the hot new (old) thing."

2015: Chef David Kinch of California's Michelin-starred Manresa develops a recipe for homemade tots that are slow-cooked in duck fat and take 12 hours to make.

2016: At the traditional pardoning of the national Thanksgiving turkey, President Obama pardons two gobblers: Tater and Tot.

2018: *TOTS!* is published, changing the course of humankind forever.

CHAPTER 4

TOT-ALLY SATISFYING

TOTS IN THE MAIN ATTRACTION

BIBIMTOT

*I*f you want to serve this recipe on a plate, that works, but using a traditional stone bowl (known as a *dolsot* in Korean—see Notes) will take this tot-sterpiece out of your open studio and into the Museum of Fine Arts. The hot bowl makes the tots super crispy, and when you stir in the runny egg yolk everything is right in the world. *SERVES 3*

1 CUP DICED RIPE PEAR

¼ CUP SOY SAUCE

¼ CUP TOASTED SESAME OIL

½ CUP DICED ONION

1 TABLESPOON GOCHUJANG CHILE PASTE (SEE NOTES)

2 TABLESPOONS HONEY

2 TABLESPOONS RICE VINEGAR

2 TABLESPOONS GRATED GARLIC

2-INCH PIECE FRESH GINGER, PEELED AND GRATED

1 POUND THINLY SHAVED BEEF (RIB EYE IS MY FAVORITE)

1 POUND FROZEN TOTS (ABOUT 45 TOTS)

3 TABLESPOONS VEGETABLE OR PEANUT OIL

NONSTICK COOKING SPRAY (OPTIONAL)

1 ZUCCHINI, SLICED INTO ¼-INCH BY 2-INCH PLANKS

1 RED BELL PEPPER, STEMMED, SEEDED, AND SLICED INTO ¼-INCH BY 2-INCH STRIPS

1 TABLESPOON UNSALTED BUTTER

3 LARGE EGGS

1 CUP KIMCHI (SEE NOTES)

SESAME SEEDS, FOR GARNISH

SRIRACHA, FOR GARNISH

1 Make a marinade: Combine the pear, soy sauce, sesame oil, onion, chile paste, honey, rice vinegar, garlic, and ginger in the bowl of a food processor, and process until smooth. Place

the beef in an airtight container or large zip-top bag, add the marinade, stir to coat, and seal. Marinate at room temperature for 1 hour, or in the refrigerator for as long as overnight.

2 When ready to make the tots, preheat the oven to 450°F.

3 Place the tots on a rimmed baking sheet and drizzle them with 2 tablespoons of the vegetable oil. Toss the tots gently to coat them evenly with the oil, then spread them out in an even layer.

4 Bake, carefully flipping the tots halfway through, until they are evenly browned and crispy, about 20 minutes. (If using stone bowls or individual cast-iron skillets, coat them lightly with cooking spray and heat them in the oven with the tots.)

5 Meanwhile, heat the remaining 1 tablespoon of vegetable oil in a grill pan, wok, or frying pan over very high heat. Add the zucchini and bell pepper and cook, turning occasionally, until the veggies are nicely browned but not overcooked,

about 5 minutes. Remove from the heat.

6 Add the beef to the pan with the vegetables and cook, stirring occasionally, to cook through and brown a little bit, about 5 minutes. Set aside.

7 Melt the butter in a nonstick frying pan over medium heat. Add the eggs and cook until starting to set on the bottom, about 3 minutes. Carefully flip with a spatula and cook until the whites are set, 1 minute more. Remove from the pan.

8 If you are using stone bowls or cast-iron skillets, remove them from the oven and add 15 tots to each, lightly pressing the tots against the wall of the bowl with a wooden spoon or heatproof spatula (be careful not to burn yourself!). If you aren't using the bowls, divide the tots among 3 plates (about 15 tots per plate).

9 Top each serving of tots with some veggies, kimchi, and beef, arranging them in a decorative pattern to give each ingredient its own little space. Place a fried egg on top in the very center of each serving.

10 Garnish with sesame seeds and sriracha and serve hot.

NOTE: Dolsots can be found at many Korean grocery stores, and some other Asian grocery stores as well. If you can't find them, substitute individual-size cast-iron pans for a similar effect.

Kimchi is a fermented vegetable dish (most often made with cabbage and radish) that's a staple of Korean cooking. Gochujang is a savory red chile paste that adds a spicy umami punch to Korean foods. You can find both at most any Korean market, and in the refrigerated section near the produce in many supermarkets.

TOTS SAAG PANEER

The classic Indian dish of mild paneer cheese smothered in a spiced spinach sauce lends itself well to the tot treatment. Smothering the tots in the sauce and topping them with fried cheese almost makes this version a crazy curried tot poutine! *SERVES 4*

- 2 TABLESPOONS (¼ STICK) UNSALTED BUTTER
- 1 LARGE ONION, DICED
- 3 JALAPEÑOS, STEMMED, SEEDED, AND DICED
- 2 GARLIC CLOVES, MINCED
- 2-INCH PIECE FRESH GINGER, PEELED AND GRATED
- 1 TEASPOON CURRY POWDER
- 1 TEASPOON GARAM MASALA
- 1 POUND FRESH BABY SPINACH
- ½ CUP PLAIN FULL-FAT YOGURT
- 2 POUNDS FROZEN TOTS (ABOUT 90 TOTS)
- 5 TABLESPOONS VEGETABLE OR PEANUT OIL
- KOSHER SALT AND FRESHLY GROUND BLACK PEPPER
- 8 OUNCES PANEER CHEESE (SEE NOTE)

1 Preheat the oven to 450°F.

2 Melt the butter in a large frying pan over low heat. Add the onion and cook, stirring occasionally, until very browned, about 30 minutes. Add the jalapeños and cook to soften slightly, about 5 minutes.

3 Add the garlic and ginger and cook, stirring occasionally, until fragrant and soft, about 3 minutes. Add the curry powder and garam masala and cook, stirring, until fragrant, about 2 minutes. Add the spinach and ½ cup of water and simmer, stirring occasionally, until all the spinach has wilted, about 10 minutes.

4 Remove from the heat and stir in the yogurt. Transfer the mixture to the bowl of a food processor and process until smooth. Taste and adjust the seasonings as needed. Return to the pan and cook over low heat until warmed through, adding water if needed to thin it out (it should have the consistency of creamed spinach). Turn off heat, cover, and keep warm until ready to use.

5 Place the frozen tots on a rimmed baking sheet and drizzle with 3 tablespoons of the oil. Toss to coat evenly with the oil and season with a pinch of salt and pepper. Bake the tots, carefully flipping them halfway through cooking, until crispy and browned, about 25 minutes.

6 Cut the cheese into 1-inch cubes. Heat the remaining 2 tablespoons oil in a large frying pan over medium-high heat, add the cheese, and cook, flipping gently with a spatula, until browned on all sides, 2 minutes per side. Remove from the pan.

7 Put the tots on a plate and top with the spinach curry sauce and the fried cheese. Serve hot.

NOTE: Paneer is becoming more common at grocery stores, but is still harder to find than most ingredients. The best bet is an Indian market. There aren't really great options to substitute, but queso blanco will work in a pinch.

LOMO SAL-TOT-O

When I first found out about *lomo saltado*, my mind was blown. You're telling me there is a classic Peruvian dish that blends South American and Asian flavors, and it has french fries mixed right in?! It sounded more like something I would throw together after being out all night than a traditional dish people have been eating for years. It was a no-brainer for me to swap out the soggy french fries for some crispy tots, taking this dish to another level. *SERVES 4*

¼ CUP RED WINE VINEGAR

2 TABLESPOONS SOY SAUCE

1 TEASPOON GROUND CUMIN

1 TEASPOON GROUND CORIANDER

KOSHER SALT AND FRESHLY
    GROUND BLACK PEPPER

1½ POUNDS SIRLOIN TIP STEAK,
    SLICED AGAINST THE GRAIN
    INTO ½-INCH-THICK STRIPS

2 POUNDS FROZEN TOTS
    (ABOUT 90 TOTS)

3 TABLESPOONS OLIVE OIL

1 RED ONION, SLICED

3 GARLIC CLOVES, MINCED

¼ CUP DICED PICKLED JALAPEÑOS

1 CAN (14 OUNCES) DICED
    TOMATOES WITH THEIR JUICES

2 CUPS COOKED WHITE RICE,
    FOR SERVING

2 TABLESPOONS CHOPPED FRESH
    CILANTRO LEAVES, FOR GARNISH

1 Preheat the oven to 450°F.

2 Combine the vinegar, soy sauce, cumin, coriander, and 1 teaspoon each of salt and pepper in a large bowl. Add the steak, stir, cover, and marinate in the fridge for 30 minutes to 1 hour.

3 Place the tots on a rimmed baking sheet (or two) and drizzle them with 2 tablespoons of the oil. Toss the tots gently to coat them evenly with the oil, then spread them out in an even layer. Bake, carefully flipping the tots once during cooking, until browned and crispy, about 25 minutes.

4 Meanwhile, heat the remaining 1 tablespoon of oil in a large frying pan over medium heat, add the onion and cook, stirring occasionally, until softened, about 5 minutes. Add the garlic and cook, stirring frequently, until it is fragrant and lightly golden, 1 minute.

5 Add the steak with its marinade. Bring the pan to a boil and cook until the beef is cooked through and the sauce has thickened slightly, about 3 minutes. Add the jalapeños and tomatoes and cook until heated through, about 3 minutes. Add the tots, stir to incorporate, and remove from the heat.

6 Serve hot over rice, garnished with cilantro.

TOT-TOPPED PIZZA

I have a lot of pizza parties. So many that I once built a brick oven in my backyard! As the pizza parties wind down, people get a little drunker, and I start to run out of ingredients, and the pizzas get more and more crazy. That's how the tot pizza was born. The reason this works, like many of the pizza combos I love, is that it has balance. The heavy, salty tots are balanced by the tart and spicy banana peppers. The condiment mixture is a natural pair for the tots and brings everything together with a last-minute drizzle. *MAKES ONE 16-INCH PIZZA; SERVES 2 TO 4*

ALL-PURPOSE FLOUR, FOR WORKING THE DOUGH

1 POUND STORE-BOUGHT REFRIGERATED PIZZA DOUGH (ENOUGH FOR 1 PIZZA)

¼ CUP OLIVE OIL

¼ CUP DICED ONION

2 GARLIC CLOVES, MINCED

1 CAN (28 OUNCES) DICED TOMATOES WITH THEIR JUICES

1 TABLESPOON DRIED OREGANO

¼ CUP GRATED PECORINO ROMANO CHEESE

KOSHER SALT AND FRESHLY GROUND BLACK PEPPER

20 FROZEN TOTS

½ TABLESPOON VEGETABLE OR PEANUT OIL

⅓ CUP MAYONNAISE

2 TABLESPOONS KETCHUP

2 TEASPOONS YELLOW MUSTARD

CORNMEAL, FOR WORKING THE DOUGH

1 CUP BANANA PEPPERS, CHOPPED

½ CUP (2 OUNCES) SHREDDED CHEDDAR CHEESE

½ CUP (2 OUNCES) SHREDDED MOZZARELLA CHEESE

1 Lightly flour a work surface and place the dough on top. Sprinkle more flour on top and cover with a clean kitchen towel. Allow to come to room temperature before using, about 1 hour.

2 Heat the olive oil in a large frying pan over medium heat. Add the onion and cook until softened, about 7 minutes. Add the garlic and cook until fragrant and lightly golden, about 2 minutes.

3 Add the tomatoes with their juices, the oregano, the pecorino cheese, and salt and pepper and simmer over medium-low heat, stirring occasionally, for 15 minutes.

4 Using a stick blender, blend the sauce until smooth. Cover the pan and set aside.

5 Preheat the oven to the highest temperature, with an oven rack set just below the broiler. Place a pizza stone, baking steel (my preference), or overturned sheet pan on the rack to preheat.

6 Meanwhile, place the tots on a rimmed baking sheet and drizzle them with the vegetable oil. Toss the tots gently to coat them evenly with the oil, then spread them out in an even layer. Warm them in the oven while it preheats, about 10 minutes.

7 Stir together the mayonnaise, ketchup, and mustard in a small bowl. Spoon the mixture into a squeeze bottle (or a zip-top bag) and set aside.

8 Sprinkle a small handful of cornmeal onto a pizza peel (or place a sheet of parchment paper on a cutting board) and put the dough round on top.

9 Remove the tots from the oven. Top the pizza dough with the sauce to taste (I usually use a heaping ½ cup of sauce), leaving the edge bare. (Leftover sauce can be stored in an airtight container in the fridge for up to 5 days, or in the freezer for up to 6 months.) Sprinkle the banana peppers over the sauce, top with the Cheddar and mozzarella cheeses, then scatter the tots evenly on top.

10 Switch the oven on high to broil. Carefully slide the pizza onto the pizza stone (if using parchment on a cutting board, you can slide the dough-topped parchment directly onto the stone) and broil, keeping an eye on it to prevent burning, until it is bubbling in the center and the tots and crust are browned, about 5 minutes.

11 Pull the pizza out of the oven and slide it onto a large cutting board.

12 Squeeze the mayonnaise mixture onto the pizza in decorative lines (if using a zip-top bag, snip a small hole in one corner to make a piping bag). Cut the pizza into slices and serve!

MOULES TOTS

oules frites are easily one of my favorite things to order at a seafood restaurant. If you eat a dish like this outdoors in the summertime, ideally with your feet in the sand or resting gently on the grass, you will remember it forever. Don't be afraid to work with mussels—they take a little while to clean, but they cook in minutes and are very inexpensive. *SERVES 3*

1 POUND FROZEN TOTS (ABOUT 45 TOTS)

3 TABLESPOONS VEGETABLE OR PEANUT OIL

KOSHER SALT

1 TABLESPOON OLIVE OIL

¼ POUND SPANISH CHORIZO, FINELY DICED (SEE NOTES)

2 CELERY RIBS, LEAVES ROUGHLY CHOPPED (TO EQUAL ¼ CUP) AND RIBS FINELY CHOPPED

2 SHALLOTS, THINLY SLICED LENGTHWISE

2½ POUNDS MUSSELS, SCRUBBED AND RINSED (SEE NOTES)

¼ CUP BANANA PEPPER RINGS

½ CUP CITRUSY, HOPPY BEER, SUCH AS IPA

¼ CUP CHOPPED FRESH ITALIAN (FLAT-LEAF) PARSLEY

JUICE OF 1 LEMON

1 Preheat the oven to 450°F.

2 Place the tots on a rimmed baking sheet, drizzle with 2 tablespoons of the vegetable oil, and sprinkle with a pinch of salt. Toss the tots gently to coat them evenly with the oil, then spread them out in an even layer. Bake, carefully flipping the tots halfway through the cooking, until crispy and browned, about 20 minutes.

3 Meanwhile, heat the olive oil in a large frying pan over medium-high heat. Add the chorizo and cook, stirring occasionally, until it has rendered a lot of its fat and is starting to crisp up, about 5 minutes. Add the chopped celery and shallots and cook, stirring occasionally, until the vegetables have softened, about 3 minutes.

4 Add the mussels and banana pepper rings and stir. Add the beer, bring it to a simmer, and cook until all of the mussels have opened, 3 to 5 minutes. (Discard any mussels that remain closed.)

5 Remove the pan from the heat and stir in the celery leaves, parsley, and lemon juice. Pour into a large, shallow bowl or a platter.

6 Serve immediately with the tots on the side to dip into all that delicious broth or, if you have a big enough bowl, dump the tots right on top of the mussels and dig in!

NOTES: Spanish chorizo can be found in the grocery store near the ham, bacon, and other cured and cooked meat products. It is sold fully cooked (like a hot dog) and has a smoky, paprika-y flavor.

To clean mussels, rinse them in cold water and pull off any strings or barnacles that are attached. Sometimes you will need to pull off the beard, which is a stringy membrane that sticks halfway out of the seam of the mussel. Grab on tight when you find one and pull it out firmly. If you find an open mussel, tap the shell with your finger and see if it closes automatically. If it doesn't close, discard that mussel.

CHICKEN TOT PIE

Chicken pot pie is one of the most classic comfort foods there is. The thing with pot pie, though, is the crust is complicated and can get soggy easily. This version uses tots as the crust, so it's easy to make and will be super crispy every time. You can make this in a large baking pan, but I like to use individual baking dishes so my guests can dig into their own little pies. *MAKES 6 INDIVIDUAL PIES*

¼ CUP PLUS 2 TABLESPOONS OLIVE OIL

1½ POUNDS BONELESS, SKINLESS CHICKEN BREASTS, CUT INTO 1-INCH CUBES

KOSHER SALT AND FRESHLY GROUND BLACK PEPPER

1 MEDIUM ONION, DICED

3 CARROTS, PEELED AND DICED

5 CELERY RIBS, DICED

3 GARLIC CLOVES, MINCED

1 QUART CHICKEN STOCK

2 TABLESPOONS (¼ STICK) SALTED BUTTER

2 TABLESPOONS HEAVY (WHIPPING) CREAM

1 TEASPOON DRIED THYME

1 CUP CHOPPED FRESH ITALIAN (FLAT-LEAF) PARSLEY LEAVES

¾ CUP POTATO FLAKES (INSTANT MASHED POTATOES)

1½ POUNDS FROZEN TOTS (ABOUT 65 TOTS)

1 Heat 1 tablespoon of the oil in a large pan over high heat, then add the chicken and cook, turning occasionally and seasoning all over with salt and pepper to taste, until browned on all sides, about 10 minutes. Transfer the chicken to a large bowl; reserve the pan.

2 Add another tablespoon of oil to the pan to coat, if needed, and add the onion, carrots, and celery. Cook over medium heat, stirring, until the vegetables have softened, about 10 minutes. Add the garlic and cook until fragrant and lightly golden, about 3 minutes. Season with salt and pepper to taste.

3 Meanwhile, use a wooden spoon to mash and shred the chicken into bite-size pieces (it's okay if there are some large chunks).

4 Add the chicken back to the pan along with the chicken stock, butter, heavy cream, thyme, and parsley. Bring to a simmer over low heat, then stir in the potato flakes to combine. Cover and remove from the heat.

5 Preheat the oven to 450°F.

6 Place the tots in a large microwave-safe bowl and microwave on high at 1-minute intervals, stirring after each, until they are defrosted and all broken up in the bowl. Add the remaining ¼ cup of olive oil and stir well until incorporated.

7 Set 6 individual baking dishes on a rimmed baking sheet and ladle the pot pie filling into them. Divide the tot mixture over the top of each dish and press down gently to flatten it into a crust. Bake until the filling bubbles out from the sides, about 30 minutes.

8 Heat the broiler to high.

9 Broil the tot pies until the crusts are browned and extra crispy, about 1 minute (watch them carefully to make sure they don't burn).

10 Let the tot pies cool slightly, then serve.

MINNESOTA HOT DISH

I knew I would have to include a recipe for Minnesota Hot Dish in a book about tots, but honestly, I was worried. First of all, it isn't exactly a "sexy" or exciting dish. (I have even seen it called "funeral casserole.") Even more than that, when I was researching the dish, EVERY recipe I found used canned cream of mushroom soup—to the extent that the authors of those recipes insisted it was essential to the dish. It simply wouldn't be Minnesota Hot Dish without it! Now I have no problem with using shortcut ingredients (hence all the frozen tots in this book), but canned cream of mushroom soup is just not for me. So I set to work making a Minnesota Hot Dish recipe that I could be proud of *and* that would do justice to the original. Here it is! *SERVES 5 OR 6*

VEGETABLE OR PEANUT OIL (OPTIONAL)

1 POUND GROUND BEEF OR TURKEY

1 MEDIUM ONION, DICED

1 CELERY RIB, DICED

4 OUNCES MUSHROOMS, TRIMMED AND DICED

2 GARLIC CLOVES, MINCED

2 CUPS SLICED GREEN BEANS, CUT INTO 1-INCH PIECES

1½ CUPS CHICKEN STOCK

1 CUP MILK

⅓ CUP POTATO FLAKES (INSTANT MASHED POTATOES)

1 POUND FROZEN TOTS (ABOUT 45 TOTS)

1   Preheat the oven to 400°F.

2   Heat a large frying pan over high heat (adding 1 tablespoon of the oil if using ground turkey). Add the ground beef and cook, stirring occasionally to break up the meat, until it is browned and cooked through, about 10 minutes. Transfer the meat to a plate and set aside.

3   Drain all but 2 tablespoons of the grease from the pan (or add more oil if necessary) and add the onion and celery. Reduce the heat to medium and cook, stirring occasionally, until the vegetables soften and the edges start to brown, about 10 minutes. Add the mushrooms and cook, stirring occasionally, until they soften, about 5 minutes. Add the garlic and cook, stirring frequently, until it is fragrant and lightly golden, about 2 minutes.

4   Return the meat to the pan and add the green beans, stock, and milk. Bring to a simmer and cook, stirring occasionally, for about 5 minutes, then whisk in the potato flakes. Bring back to a simmer and cook, stirring occasionally, until the mixture starts to thicken, 2 minutes more.

5   Pour the mixture into an 11 x 7-inch casserole dish, spreading it into an even layer. Top with the tots and bake until the tots are browned on top and the filling is bubbling out from the sides, about 30 minutes. Serve hot.

SHEPHERD'S PIE *with* A TOTTY TOP

I grew up eating an Irish-American version of shepherd's pie, which is drier than the British version, with lamb on the bottom, corn in the middle, and potato on top. I also ate a ton of British-style shepherd's pies—which are more like gravy-based stew topped with potatoes—when I lived in Bermuda. For this version I sort of combined the two to make my own style, and bastardized it even further by using beef instead of lamb—and then topping it with tots! So here is a delicious recipe for an Irish-American-British Tot- and Cheese-Topped Beef Shepherd's Pie!

SERVES 5 OR 6

1 TEASPOON VEGETABLE OR PEANUT OIL

1 POUND GROUND BEEF (OR LAMB)

1 MEDIUM ONION, PEELED AND DICED

2 MEDIUM CARROTS, PEELED AND DICED

2 GARLIC CLOVES, MINCED

1 CAN (28 OUNCES) DICED TOMATOES WITH THEIR JUICES

1 CUP CORN KERNELS (FRESH OR FROZEN)

2 TABLESPOONS WORCESTERSHIRE SAUCE

2 TABLESPOONS RED WINE VINEGAR

2 TEASPOONS CHOPPED FRESH THYME

ABOUT 1 POUND FROZEN TOTS (DEPENDING ON THE SIZE OF YOUR BAKING DISHES)

1 CUP (4 OUNCES) SHREDDED CHEDDAR CHEESE

1 Preheat the oven to 400°F.

2 Heat the oil in a large frying pan over high heat. Add the ground beef and cook, stirring occasionally to break up the meat, until it is browned and cooked through, about 15 minutes. Transfer the meat to a plate, leaving the fat in the pan.

3 Add the onion and carrots to the pan and cook over medium heat, stirring occasionally, until softened and lightly browned, about 15 minutes. Add the garlic and cook, stirring frequently, until fragrant and lightly golden, about 2 minutes.

4 Add the tomatoes, corn, Worcestershire sauce, vinegar, and thyme and stir to combine. Return the beef to the pan, bring the mixture to a simmer, and cook until the flavors have melded and the mixture thickens slightly, about 15 minutes.

5 Pour the beef mixture into an 11 x 7-inch casserole dish or divide it among 5 or 6 individual baking dishes. Top the beef mixture with the tots, covering it evenly and making sure the tots don't sink too far into the dish.

6 Bake until the tots are golden brown on top, about 30 minutes.

7 Remove the shepherd's pie(s) from the oven, top with the cheese, and bake until the cheese has melted and the filling is bubbling at the edges, about 10 minutes.

8 Let cool for 10 minutes, then serve.

MAC 'N' TOT 'N' CHEESE

Potatoes go better in mac and cheese than most people expect. Cheese, potatoes, and pasta. What's not to love? I like to add a little kale to this dish and serve it with pickled onions to cut the richness a bit.

FYI: The pickled onions can be made a few weeks in advance, and the mac and cheese can be refrigerated, unbaked, in the casserole dish for up to 3 days—just add 30 minutes to the bake time. *SERVES 8*

FOR THE PICKLED ONIONS

1 SMALL RED ONION, THINLY SLICED

2 GARLIC CLOVES, PEELED

1 TEASPOON WHOLE MUSTARD SEEDS

1 TEASPOON BLACK PEPPERCORNS

1 TEASPOON KOSHER SALT

1 TEASPOON SUGAR

1 CUP RED WINE VINEGAR

FOR THE MAC AND CHEESE

1 TABLESPOON KOSHER SALT, PLUS EXTRA AS NEEDED

4 TABLESPOONS (½ STICK) UNSALTED BUTTER

4 TABLESPOONS ALL-PURPOSE FLOUR

5 CUPS WHOLE MILK

1 BUNCH KALE, STEMS REMOVED AND LEAVES FINELY CHOPPED

1 POUND DRIED SMALL PASTA (I LIKE USING CELLENTANI)

1 BLOCK (16 OUNCES) CHEDDAR CHEESE, SHREDDED

1 BLOCK (16 OUNCES) MONTEREY JACK CHEESE, SHREDDED

1½ POUNDS FROZEN TOTS (ABOUT 65 TOTS)

1 Make the pickled onions: Place the onion in a pint-size heatproof jar with a lid (such as a Mason jar) and add the garlic, mustard seeds, peppercorns, salt, and sugar.

2 Stir the vinegar and ½ cup of water together in a microwave-safe bowl. Microwave on high until very hot and steaming, about 3 minutes.

3 Pour the vinegar mixture over the onion mixture, adding a little more water if needed to cover the onions. Cover and allow to sit at room temperature for 1 hour, then refrigerate until cool. (The pickled onions will keep, in an airtight container in the refrigerator, for a few weeks.)

4 Make the mac and cheese: Fill a large pot with water, add 1 tablespoon of salt, and bring to a boil over high heat.

5 Meanwhile, melt the butter in a large, heavy-bottomed saucepan or a Dutch oven over medium heat. Add the flour and cook, stirring constantly, until it darkens by one or two shades to a golden color, about 3 minutes. Add the milk and whisk well to combine. Bring to a simmer over medium heat and cook, stirring often so the milk doesn't stick to the bottom of the pot and burn, until the sauce thickens slightly. Kill the heat and stir in the kale.

6 Add the pasta to the boiling water and cook until it is very al dente (it should still have a real bite to it because it will continue to cook in the oven).

7 Drain the pasta and add it to the sauce along with the Cheddar and Monterey Jack cheeses. Stir well until the cheeses are incorporated and the pasta is coated evenly. Stir in half of the tots. Add salt to taste.

8 Transfer the pasta mixture to a 9 x 13-inch baking dish and top with the remaining tots. Bake until the tots are crispy and the mac and cheese is bubbling, about 30 minutes. Serve hot, with the pickled onions alongside.

KENTUCKY TOT HOT BROWN

This indulgent open-face sandwich from Kentucky is smothered in a cheesy Mornay sauce and broiled until crispy. Serving it on a large tot instead of bread gives this traditionally soggy mess a much-needed crispy element and a new dimension of flavor. *MAKES 4 OPEN-FACE SANDWICHES; SERVES 2 TO 4*

FOR THE MORNAY SAUCE

- 2 TABLESPOONS (¼ STICK) (UNSALTED BUTTER
- ¼ CUP GRATED ONION (ABOUT HALF A SMALL ONION)
- 2 TABLESPOONS ALL-PURPOSE FLOUR
- 1½ CUPS WHOLE MILK
- ½ CUP GRATED PARMESAN CHEESE
- ½ CUP SHREDDED SHARP WHITE CHEDDAR CHEESE
- PINCH OF SWEET PAPRIKA

FOR THE SANDWICHES

- 4 FROZEN MONSTER TOTS (AKA HASH BROWN PATTIES)
- 4 SLICES ROASTED TURKEY (PREFERABLY FRESH INSTEAD OF DELI TURKEY)
- 1 TOMATO, SLICED
- ¼ CUP GRATED PARMESAN CHEESE
- 4 BACON STRIPS, COOKED UNTIL CRISPY

1 Make the Mornay sauce:
Melt the butter in a medium saucepan over medium heat. Add the onion and cook, stirring occasionally, until softened, about 5 minutes.

2 Whisk in the flour, whisking well to combine, and cook, whisking constantly so no flour sticks to the bottom of the pan, until the mixture is a light golden color, about 3 minutes.

3 Whisk in the milk and bring to a simmer, whisking often. Once it starts simmering and you notice the sauce thickening, about 5 minutes, remove the pan from heat. Immediately whisk in the Parmesan, Cheddar, and paprika until combined. Cover the pan and set aside.

4 Make the sandwiches:
Preheat the broiler to high.

Place the hash brown patties on a rimmed baking sheet and broil, watching carefully to make sure they don't burn, until browned on top, about 5 minutes. Flip the patties with a spatula and broil until brown on the opposite side, 3 to 5 minutes more.

5 Layer the patties in the bottom of an oven-safe dish (or individual dishes). Top each patty with a turkey slice, then about ¼ cup of the Mornay sauce. Next, evenly divide the tomato slices among each sandwich. Add more sauce, and then the Parmesan.

6 Broil until the sauce browns in spots, about 3 minutes.

7 Remove from the oven, top each sandwich with the bacon, and serve immediately.

MONSTER TOT BACON GRILLED CHEESE

Grilled cheese with tots as the bread! There isn't much else to say. Except bacon! *SERVES 1*

- 1 TABLESPOON VEGETABLE OR PEANUT OIL, FOR FRYING
- 2 FROZEN MONSTER TOTS (AKA HASH BROWN PATTIES)
- 3 SLICES AMERICAN CHEESE
- 2 BACON STRIPS, COOKED UNTIL CRISPY

1 Pour the oil into a large frying pan and heat it over medium heat. Add the tots and cook on one side until lightly browned, about 5 minutes. Using a spatula, flip the tots very gently and cook on the second side to a darker brown, about 5 minutes more.

2 Turn the heat down to low. Flip one of the tots so the darker brown side is facing up. Top with 2 slices of the cheese, then the bacon and the remaining slice of cheese. Place the second tot on top, browner side down. Press gently.

3 Cover the sandwich and cook until the cheese has softened, about 1 minute. Very gently flip the sandwich with the spatula. Cover and cook until the cheese has melted, about 1 minute more.

4 Remove the sandwich from the pan, slice it in half, and serve immediately.

FISH IN CHIPS

The combination of crispy potatoes and tender flaky fish will never go out of style. Tots make this traditionally challenging dish much easier to prepare because of their built-in crispness. *SERVES 4*

32 FROZEN TOTS

1 LARGE EGG WHITE

¼ CUP ALL-PURPOSE FLOUR

PINCH OF KOSHER SALT

4 HADDOCK FILLETS
(4 TO 6 OUNCES EACH)

¼ CUP DIJON MUSTARD

UNSALTED BUTTER,
FOR COOKING THE FISH

1 Place the tots in a large microwave-safe bowl and microwave on high at 1-minute intervals, stirring after each, until defrosted and broken down, about 5 minutes total. Stir the egg white into the tots to incorporate, and set the bowl aside.

2 Place the flour in a shallow bowl and stir in the salt. Lightly dredge the top of each fish fillet through the flour mixture to coat it very lightly. Set the coated fillets on a plate and brush a tablespoon of mustard on top of each.

3 Mound some of the tot mixture on top of each fillet, dividing it equally among them and pressing it on firmly so it sticks.

4 Melt a generous knob of butter in a large, nonstick frying pan or cast-iron skillet over medium-high heat. Carefully add the fillets, tot-side down, and cook until the tot mixture is brown, about 6 minutes. Carefully flip each fillet with a spatula and continue to cook until the fish is cooked through, 3 to 5 minutes more.

5 Serve immediately.

TOTS-GIVING STUFFING

Tots are a natural bread replacement in this twist on a classic stuffing. When creating this recipe, I was inspired by a meat stuffing that my grandmother used to make that was loaded with potatoes. It's a fun and delicious addition to any Thanksgiving or Friendsgiving table, and as a bonus, it's a bread-free version of stuffing that most everyone can enjoy! *SERVES 10*

1 POUND SWEET ITALIAN SAUSAGE, REMOVED FROM THE CASINGS

1 CUP DICED ONION

1 CUP DICED CARROT

1 CUP DICED CELERY

1 GARLIC CLOVE, MINCED

PINCH OF DRIED ROSEMARY LEAVES

PINCH OF DRIED SAGE LEAVES

½ CUP CHOPPED FRESH ITALIAN (FLAT-LEAF) PARSLEY LEAVES

2 POUNDS FROZEN TOTS (ABOUT 90 TOTS)

2 CUPS CHICKEN STOCK

2 LARGE EGGS

½ CUP POTATO FLAKES (INSTANT MASHED POTATOES)

1 Preheat the oven to 350°F.

2 Place the sausage in a large frying pan over high heat and cook, stirring occasionally to break up the meat, until the sausage is browned and cooked through, about 10 minutes. Transfer the sausage to a large bowl and drain all but 2 tablespoons of the fat in the pan.

3 Add the onion, carrot, and celery to the pan and cook over medium heat until softened, about 10 minutes. Add the garlic, rosemary, and sage and cook, stirring often, until the garlic is fragrant and lightly golden, about 2 minutes.

4 Add the onion mixture to the sausage in the bowl. Add the parsley and the frozen tots and stir gently to combine. In another bowl, whisk together the stock, eggs, and potato flakes to incorporate. Add this mixture to the sausage mixture and stir well.

5 Pour the stuffing mixture into a 9 x 13-inch baking dish and bake until heated through and crispy on top, 45 minutes.

6 Serve hot.

Tots-giving Stuffing will keep, covered in the refrigerator, for 4 days. Reheat it in a 350° oven until warmed through.

CHAPTER 5

SWEET TOTS FOR YOUR SWEET TOOTH

TOTS DO DESSERT

APPLE TOT CRISP

A warm apple crisp can really hit the spot when the weather first turns chilly in late September. Something about the play between the tender and sweet apples and the crispy oat topping warms the soul that time of year. I bet you can guess what I am going to say next. The crispy, salty tots really enhance the topping and add something unique to this dessert! *SERVES 6*

FOR THE FILLING

7 APPLES (I LIKE TO USE
    4 HONEYCRISP AND
    3 BRAEBURN)

⅓ CUP DARK BROWN SUGAR

1 TABLESPOON CORNSTARCH

JUICE OF 1 LEMON

1 TEASPOON GROUND CINNAMON

PINCH OF GROUND NUTMEG

1 TEASPOON PURE VANILLA
    EXTRACT

½ TEASPOON KOSHER SALT

FOR THE TOPPING AND SERVING

1 POUND FROZEN TOTS
    (ABOUT 45 TOTS)

1 CUP OLD-FASHIONED
    (ROLLED) OATS

1 TEASPOON GROUND CINNAMON

6 TABLESPOONS (¾ STICK)
    UNSALTED BUTTER,
    AT ROOM TEMPERATURE

⅓ CUP DARK BROWN SUGAR

VANILLA ICE CREAM, FOR SERVING

1 Preheat the oven to 350°F.

2 Make the filling: Peel and core the apples and cut them into ¾-inch cubes. Place them in a large bowl and add the brown sugar, cornstarch, lemon juice, cinnamon, nutmeg, vanilla, and salt. Toss to coat, then pour the apples into an 11 x 7-inch baking dish.

3 Make the topping: Place the tots in a large microwave-safe bowl and defrost in the microwave on high, pausing to stir and break them up, about 4 minutes. Pour the tots into a large bowl and add the oats, cinnamon, and butter. Stir well to combine.

4 Spread the tot mixture in an even layer on top of the apples in the baking dish and sprinkle the brown sugar on top.

5 Bake until browned and crispy on top, about 50 minutes.

6 Allow to cool slightly, then serve with vanilla ice cream.

Apple Tot Crisp will keep, covered in the refrigerator, for 2 to 3 days. Reheat it in a 350°F oven before serving.

TOT CHURROS

The crispy-on-the-outside, tender-on-the-inside texture of a churro lends itself well to the tot treatment. Unlike some other tot recipes, this one must be fried and not baked in order to give the tots that hot and crispy carnival-food feel. Lots and lots of cinnamon and the warm chocolate ganache dipping sauce complete the churro transformation. *SERVES 5*

¼ CUP HEAVY (WHIPPING) CREAM

1 CUP BITTERSWEET CHOCOLATE CHIPS

KOSHER SALT

2 TABLESPOONS GROUND CINNAMON

½ CUP SUGAR

VEGETABLE OR PEANUT OIL, FOR FRYING

1 POUND FROZEN TOTS (ABOUT 45 TOTS)

1 Combine the heavy cream, chocolate, and a pinch of salt in a microwave-safe bowl and microwave on high at 30-second intervals, stirring after each, just until the chocolate has melted and the mixture is combined. Be careful not to overheat. Set the ganache aside.

2 Stir together the cinnamon, sugar, and a pinch of salt in a large bowl.

3 Pour oil to a depth of 4 inches into a large, heavy-bottomed pot. Heat the oil over medium-high heat until a deep-fry or candy thermometer inserted into the oil reaches 375°F.

4 Add the tots to the oil and fry until golden brown and crispy, about 4 minutes.

5 Using a slotted spoon, immediately transfer the tots to the cinnamon sugar mixture and toss them gently to coat.

6 Serve the Tot Churros immediately, with the chocolate ganache alongside for dipping.

RUM-GLAZED DONUTS
with TOT-BACON CRUNCH

Donuts are really popular right now and I honestly can't get enough. Any hipster donut shop worth its salt will have a bacon donut on the menu, but adding tots gives these donuts a crazy crunch and an awesome look. *MAKES 10 DONUTS*

FOR THE DONUTS

¾ CUP WHOLE MILK

4 TABLESPOONS (½ STICK) UNSALTED BUTTER, PLUS EXTRA FOR COATING THE BOWL

⅓ CUP WARM WATER (IT SHOULD BE ABOUT 100°F—ROUGHLY BODY TEMPERATURE)

1 PACKET (¼ OUNCE) ACTIVE DRY YEAST

¼ CUP SUGAR

2 LARGE EGGS

3½ CUPS ALL-PURPOSE FLOUR, PLUS EXTRA FOR COATING THE WORK SURFACE

VEGETABLE OR PEANUT OIL, FOR FRYING

FOR THE GLAZE

4 TABLESPOONS (½ STICK) UNSALTED BUTTER

½ CUP PURE MAPLE SYRUP

¼ CUP DARK RUM

ABOUT 1 CUP CONFECTIONERS' SUGAR

FOR THE TOPPING

NONSTICK COOKING SPRAY

20 FROZEN TOTS

4 BACON STRIPS

1. Make the donut batter: Combine the milk and butter in a microwave-safe bowl and microwave on high at 1-minute intervals, stirring after each, until the butter is melted and mixed into the milk.

2. Place the warm water in a large bowl and stir in the yeast. Allow to sit 10 minutes to activate.

3. Add the butter mixture to the yeast mixture. Whisk in the sugar and eggs to combine. Add half of the flour and stir with a wooden spoon to combine. Add the remaining flour and stir to combine.

4. Lightly flour a work surface and scrape the dough out onto it. Knead the dough until smooth, about 7 minutes.

5. Coat the inside of a large, clean bowl with butter, and place the dough in it. Cover with a clean kitchen towel and let rest in a warm place until doubled in size, about 1 hour.

6. Make the glaze: Combine the butter and maple syrup in a small saucepan over high heat and bring to a boil. Carefully add the rum, stir in, and continue to boil for about 1 minute. Remove from the heat and whisk in the confectioners' sugar, in batches, until the mixture has thickened and coats the back of a spoon.

7. Make the topping: Preheat the oven to 400°F. Lightly coat a rimmed baking sheet with cooking spray.

8. Place the tots in a microwave-safe bowl and microwave on high at 1-minute intervals, stirring after each, until defrosted. Break the tots into small pieces. Spread the tot pieces on the prepared baking sheet and bake, stirring every 5 minutes or so, until evenly browned and crispy, about 20 minutes. Transfer to a large bowl.

9. Meanwhile, cook the bacon in a frying pan over medium heat until crispy, about 7 minutes. Transfer to a plate and pat off the excess grease with a paper towel. Crumble the bacon into the tots and stir to combine. Set aside.

10. After the dough has risen, lightly flour a work surface and place the dough on it. Knead it gently for 1 minute, then roll it out to a ½-inch

thickness. Use 2 round cutters, one larger and one smaller, to cut out the classic donut shape. (I use a pint glass and a shot glass, respectively.) Continue until you have all the donuts cut, and reroll the remaining dough to finish out all 10 donuts (or just cut the remaining scraps into donut holes). Cover the cut dough with a clean kitchen towel and let it rest for 30 minutes (the donuts will rise a little).

11 When the dough has rested for 20 minutes, heat the frying oil: Pour oil to a depth of 2 inches into a large, heavy-bottomed pot. Heat the oil over medium-high heat until a deep-fry or candy thermometer inserted into the oil reaches 375°F. Set a cooling rack over a layer of paper towels.

12 Fry the donuts in 3 batches, turning once with tongs, until they turn a light golden color, about 1 minute per side. Transfer them to the cooling rack and let cool for 15 minutes.

13 Drizzle the cooled donuts with the glaze, then dip them, glaze-side down, into the reserved tot-bacon mixture to form the topping. Serve immediately.

TOT-AL ECLAIRS OF THE HEART

I love pastry cream as it is, but mixing sweet potato tots into it gives it a new texture and unique flavor. That plus a little cinnamon and a dark chocolate ganache make these heart-shape éclairs easy to love. *MAKES 14 ECLAIRS*

~~~~~~

FOR THE PASTRY CREAM

20 FROZEN SWEET POTATO TOTS

2 CUPS WHOLE MILK

5 LARGE EGG YOLKS

½ CUP SUGAR

⅓ CUP CORNSTARCH

2 TABLESPOONS (¼ STICK) UNSALTED BUTTER

1 TEASPOON PURE VANILLA EXTRACT

PINCH OF GROUND CINNAMON

FOR THE DOUGH

½ CUP (1 STICK) UNSALTED BUTTER, PLUS EXTRA FOR GREASING THE BAKING SHEET

¼ TEASPOON KOSHER SALT

1 CUP ALL-PURPOSE FLOUR

4 LARGE EGGS

FOR THE GANACHE

1 CUP SEMISWEET CHOCOLATE CHIPS

¼ CUP HEAVY (WHIPPING) CREAM

PINCH OF KOSHER SALT

1 Make the pastry cream: Place the tots and milk in a medium-size saucepan over medium heat. Bring to a simmer and cook, stirring occasionally, until the tots have defrosted and broken down, about 5 minutes. Remove from the heat.

2 Combine the egg yolks and sugar in a large bowl and whisk until the mixture has lightened in color, about 2 minutes. Whisk in the cornstarch.

3 Whisk one fourth of the tot mixture into the egg mixture until incorporated (this will temper the eggs), then pour this mixture into the saucepan with the remaining tot mixture. Bring to a full boil over medium-high heat, then remove from the heat. Stir in the butter, vanilla, and cinnamon until combined.

4 Pour the pastry cream into a bowl and cover it with plastic wrap directly touching the surface of the cream. Refrigerate for at least 3 hours or up to overnight.

5 Make the dough: Preheat the oven to 450°F. Grease a rimmed baking sheet with butter and line it with parchment paper.

6 Combine the ½ cup butter with 1 cup of water and the salt in a medium-size saucepan and bring to a boil over medium-high heat. Remove from the heat and vigorously stir in the flour with a wooden spoon, making sure there are no lumps. Return to medium-high heat and cook, stirring well while scraping the bottom to make sure nothing sticks, until the dough looks smooth, about 45 seconds.

7 Transfer the dough to the bowl of a stand mixer or to a large bowl if using a handheld electric mixer. Beat in the eggs, one at a time, adding the next egg only when the previous one is fully incorporated.

8 Put the dough into a piping bag with a 1-inch-diameter opening (or in a large zip-top bag, snipping off a corner). Pipe the dough into V shapes on the prepared baking sheet, about 3 inches apart. Each line of the V should be about 3 inches long; they will bake up to look like hearts.

9 Bake for 10 minutes, then reduce the heat to 350°F and bake until puffed and lightly golden, about 20 minutes more.

10 Remove the baking sheet from the oven, transfer the eclairs to a cooling rack, and allow to cool completely.

11 Make the ganache: Combine the chocolate chips, cream, and salt in a microwave-safe bowl and microwave on medium at 30-second intervals, stirring after each, just until the chocolate has melted and the mixture is combined. Be careful not to overheat.

12 Assemble the éclairs: Scoop the pastry cream into a piping bag with a wide metal tip (or into a large zip-top bag, snipping off a corner), filling the bag halfway (you can refill it when it gets low). Pipe the pastry cream into each eclair: Poke a small hole in each end of the pastry with the piping tip (or the tip of a knife if using a zip-top) and squeeze in the cream, filling it until some of the filling starts coming out of the hole.

13 Spread a tablespoonful of ganache on the top of each éclair to coat. Set the éclairs aside to set the ganache, about 30 minutes.

14 Serve right away—the éclairs taste best fresh.

NOTE: If you want to make the éclairs in advance, store the shells and cream separately and fill the shells as needed. The pastry cream will keep, in an airtight container in the refrigerator, for up to 3 days; the pastry shells will keep, in an airtight container at room temperature, for up to 3 days.

SWEET PO-TOT-O PIE

This was the first dessert I made for this book and I truly didn't expect it to be good. I'm glad I was wrong! I have made it many times since then because it is so easy and so delicious. This pie has the earthy spice you expect from sweet potato, and a nice depth of flavor from the creamy toasted marshmallow. *SERVES 10*

20 OUNCES SWEET POTATO TOTS

2 LARGE EGGS

¾ CUP SUGAR

4 TABLESPOONS (½ STICK) UNSALTED BUTTER, MELTED

1 TEASPOON GROUND CINNAMON

1 TEASPOON PURE VANILLA EXTRACT

PINCH OF GROUND NUTMEG

FROZEN 9-INCH DEEP-DISH PIECRUST (OR YOUR FAVORITE PIECRUST)

1 CUP MINI MARSHMALLOWS

VANILLA ICE CREAM, FOR SERVING (OPTIONAL)

1 Preheat the oven to 350°F with an oven rack in the top position.

2 Place half of the tots in a microwave-safe bowl and microwave on high for about about 2 minutes, pausing occasionally to stir, until the tots have defrosted and broken apart.

3 Combine the eggs and sugar in a large bowl and whisk together until the mixture has lightened in color, about 3 minutes. Whisk in the butter, then add the cinnamon, vanilla, and nutmeg and whisk to combine. Stir in the mashed tots with a wooden spoon until fully combined.

4 Pour the tot mixture into the piecrust. Top the tot mixture with the remaining whole tots, then place the marshmallows on top.

5 Bake the pie until the filling is set and the marshmallows are browned, about 50 minutes.

6 Allow to cool for 20 minutes. Serve warm with vanilla ice cream, if you like.

Sweet Po-tot-o Pie will keep, covered in the refrigerator, for up to 3 days. Let it come to room temperature before serving.

SALTED CARAMEL TOT COOKIES

When you hand someone a tot cookie and tell them what it is, they might think they misheard you. You can actually see them puzzling over it. "What did you say?" they might ask. "A tot cookie," you will reply. They might be hesitant to try it. After the first bite though, their hesitation will melt away and they will come back for more. These tot cookies are amazing: crunchy, chewy, salty, and sweet. *MAKES 24 COOKIES*

NONSTICK COOKING SPRAY, FOR COATING THE BAKING SHEET

20 FROZEN TOTS

3 CUPS SIFTED ALL-PURPOSE FLOUR

1 TEASPOON BAKING POWDER

½ TEASPOON BAKING SODA

1 TEASPOON KOSHER SALT

1¼ CUPS (2½ STICKS) UNSALTED BUTTER, AT ROOM TEMPERATURE

1 CUP LIGHT OR DARK BROWN SUGAR

½ CUP SUGAR

2 LARGE EGGS

2 TEASPOONS PURE VANILLA EXTRACT

1 CUP CARAMEL BITS (OR CHOPPED CARAMELS)

1 CUP SEMISWEET CHOCOLATE CHIPS

1 Preheat the oven to 450°F. Lightly coat a rimmed baking sheet with cooking spray.

2 Place the tots in a microwave-safe bowl and microwave on high, pausing occasionally to stir, until defrosted, about 2 minutes. Mash up the tots until they are fully broken up.

3 Spread the tot pieces onto the prepared baking sheet. Bake, stirring every 10 minutes or so, until all the tot bits are browned up and very crispy, about 25 minutes total. (Make sure to break up any bigger chunks each time you stir.) Transfer to a plate and let cool.

4 Reduce the oven temperature to 350°F. Line the baking sheet with parchment paper.

5 Stir together the flour, baking powder, baking soda, and salt in a large bowl.

6 Beat the butter and sugars together in large bowl with an electric mixer on medium-high speed, until the mixture lightens in color and is fluffy, about 4 minutes. Add the eggs and beat until incorporated. Beat in the vanilla.

7 Pour the butter mixture into the flour mixture and beat on medium speed until combined.

8 Using a wooden spoon, stir in the caramel, chocolate, and tot pieces until combined.

9 Scoop the dough in heaping tablespoon portions onto the prepared baking sheet, spacing them about 3 inches apart.

10 Bake until the cookies are pale golden all over and crispy at the edges (they will be chewy and delicious in the centers), about 12 minutes.

Salted Caramel Tot Cookies will keep, in an airtight container at room temperature, for 4 to 5 days.

S'MORES TOTS

I first wanted to make this into a tot s'more sandwich somehow, but none of the versions I tried seemed to be worth the effort or better than the standard s'more. So I gave up and threw all the ingredients into a pan. Then I took a bite and it was amazing. *SERVES 6*

1½ POUNDS FROZEN TOTS
  (ABOUT 65 TOTS)

2 TABLESPOONS VEGETABLE OR
  PEANUT OIL

1 SLEEVE GRAHAM CRACKERS
  (9 WHOLE SHEETS)

1 CUP SUGAR

1 CUP SEMISWEET CHOCOLATE
  CHIPS

1 CUP MINI MARSHMALLOWS

1 Preheat the oven to 450°F.

2 Place the tots on a rimmed baking sheet and drizzle them with the oil. Toss the tots gently to coat them evenly with the oil, then spread them out in an even layer.

3 Bake the tots, flipping them with a spatula halfway through cooking, until evenly browned and crispy, about 25 minutes.

4 Meanwhile, place the graham crackers and sugar in the bowl of a food processor and process until smooth.

5 When the tots come out of the oven, immediately put them in a large bowl and pour the graham cracker mixture on top. Toss to coat.

6 Pile the coated tots into a 12-inch cast-iron skillet or onto the center of a parchment-lined rimmed baking sheet, reserving any bits of graham

cracker mixture that remain in the bowl. Top the tots with the chocolate and marshmallows, then sprinkle the reserved graham cracker mixture on top.

7 Bake until the marshmallows brown on top and the chocolate melts, about 10 minutes.

8 Serve immediately, using forks (or your fingers if you're brave) to eat the tots right out of the pan.

TOT YA LATER!

INDEX

Note: Page references in *italics* indicate photographs.

A

Aioli, 31–32
Apple:
  tot crisp, 132–33
  veggie tots, 11–12
Avocados:
  breakfast bur-tot-o, 74–75
  guacamole, 23–24

B

Bacon:
  baked potato tots, 12
  and caramelized onion, tot crust quiche with, 81–82
  cheesy tot skins, 61–62
  Kentucky tot hot brown, 122–23
  loaded tots, 25–26
  monster tot grilled cheese, *124*, 125
  totapeño poppers, 48, *49*
  -tot crunch, rum-glazed donuts with, *136*, 137–39
  -wrapped tots, 42, *43*
Bahn mi tots, 33
Baked potato tots, 12
Beef:
  bibimtot, *96*, 97–99
  cheeseburger tots, 33

cheeseburger tot sliders, 67–68, *69*
cheesesteak tots, 33
corned, hash tots, 12
grilled, tots, 33
lomo sal-tot-o, 102–3
Minnesota hot dish, 114–15
reuben tots, 33
shepherd's pie with a totty top, *116*, 117–18
sloppy tots, 33
stroganoff tots, 33
taco tots, 12
tot Bolognese, 33
tot-co spring rolls, 53–54
Beet veggie tots, 11
Bibimtot, *96*, 97–99
Broccoli veggie tots, 11
Buffalo tots, 29–30

C

Cacio e pepe tots, 13–14
Caesar, tot, *34*, 35–36
Cauliflower veggie tots, 11
Caviar and sour cream, totkes with, 45–47, *46*
Cheese:
  baked potato tots, 12
  buffalo tots, 29–30
  cacio e pepe tots, 13–14
  cheeseburger tots, 33
  cheeseburger tot sliders, 67–68, *69*
  cheesesteak tots, 33

cheesy tot skins, 61–62
chili cheese tots, 33
grilled, monster tot bacon, *124*, 125
Kentucky tot hot brown, 122–23
loaded tots, 25–26
mac 'n' tot 'n,' 119–20, *121*
Mornay sauce, 122–23
pizza tots, 33
sauce, spicy, *15*, 16–17
sloppy tots, 33
spinach-tot dip, 50
taco tots, 12
toaster pizza tots, 44
totapeño poppers, 48, *49*
tot Bolognese, 33
tot Caesar, *34*, 35–36
totchos, *22*, 23–24
tot-co spring rolls, 53–54
tot crust quiche with bacon and caramelized onion, 81–82
tot migas, 79–80
tot-rogi, 59–60
tots à la Huancaina, 37–38, *39*
tots poutine, 27–28
tots saag paneer, 100–101
tot-stuffed mushrooms, 63–64
tot-stuffed pork meatballs with spicy romesco sauce, 55, 56–58

tot-topped pizza, 104–7, 105
totzarella sticks, 65–66
veggie tots, 10–11
Chicken:
  coated in tots and deep-fried, 66
  tot pie, 111–12, 113
  and tot-waffles, 86–89, 88
Chile peppers:
  chipotle mayo, 15, 16
  pico de gallo, 23–24
  spicy cheese sauce, 15, 16–17
  spicy romesco sauce, 55, 56–58
  totapeño poppers, 48, 49
  totchos, 22, 23–24
  tot-co spring rolls, 53–54
  tots à la Huancaina, 37–38, 39
  tots saag paneer, 100–101
Chili cheese tots, 33
Chimichurri, 15, 18–19
Chipotle mayo, 15, 16
Chive(s):
  baked potato tots, 12
  cheesy tot skins, 61–62
  chimichurri, 15, 18–19
  and garlic tots, 14
  loaded tots, 25–26
  onion dip, 15, 17–18
Chocolate:
  salted caramel tot cookies, 147–49, 148
  s'mores tots, 150–52, 151
  tot-al éclairs of the heart, 140–43, 141
  tot churros, 134–35
Chowder tots, 33
Churros, tot, 134–35
Cilantro:
  pico de gallo, 23–24

tot-co spring rolls, 53–54
Clams, in chowder tots, 33
Cookies, salted caramel tot, 147–49, 148
Corned beef hash tots, 12
Country-fried tots, 33

D

Desserts:
  apple tot crisp, 132–33
  rum-glazed donuts with tot-bacon crunch, 136, 137–39
  salted caramel tot cookies, 147–49, 148
  s'mores tots, 150–52, 151
  sweet po-tot-o pie, 144, 145–46
  tot-al éclairs of the heart, 140–43, 141
  tot churros, 134–35
Deviled tots, 70–71
Dips:
  aioli, 31–32
  guacamole, 23–24
  onion, 15, 17–18
  spinach-tot, 50
Donuts, rum-glazed, with tot-bacon crunch, 136, 137–39

E

Éclairs, tot-al, of the heart, 140–43, 141
Eggs:
  adding to tots poutine, 28
  bahn mi tots, 33
  bibimtot, 96, 97–99
  breakfast bur-tot-o, 74–75
  country-fried tots, 33
  not your Aunt Sandy's po-tot-o salad, 40–41
  sc-tot-ch, 90–91

toad in a tot hole, 92
tot crust quiche with bacon and caramelized onion, 81–82
tot migas, 79–80
tots à la Huancaina, 37–38, 39
tots Benedict, 76, 77–78
tot shakshuka, 83–84, 85

F

Fish:
  in chips, 126
  coated in tots and deep-fried, 66
Flavor boosters, 12

G

Garlic:
  aioli, 31–32
  and chive tots, 14
Ginger sesame tots, 14–16
Greek tots, 33
Green beans, in Minnesota hot dish, 114–15
Grilled beef tots, 33
Guacamole, 23–24

H

Ham, in tots Benedict, 76, 77–78
Herbs:
  chimichurri, 15, 18–19
  rosemary truffle tots, 13
  see also Chive(s)
Homemade tots, 9–10
Horseradish sauce, 15, 19

K

Kale, in mac 'n' tot 'n' cheese, 119–20, 121
Kentucky tot hot brown, 122–23

L

Lamb:
  Greek tots, 33
  shepherd's pie with a
    totty top, *116*, 117–18
Lettuce, in tot Caesar, *34*,
  35–36
Loaded tots, 25–26
Lobster roll tots, 33
Lomo sal-tot-o, 102–3

M

Mac and cheese, coated in
  tots and deep-fried,
  66
Mac 'n' tot 'n' cheese,
  119–20, *121*
Marshmallows:
  s'mores tots, 150–
    52, *151*
  sweet po-tot-o pie,
    144, 145–46
Mayonnaise:
  aioli, 31–32
  chipotle, *15*, 16
Meatballs, tot-stuffed pork,
  with spicy romesco
  sauce, 55, 56–58
Migas, tot, 79–80
Minnesota hot dish, 114–15
Monster tot bacon grilled
  cheese, *124*, 125
Mornay sauce, 122–23
Moules tots, *108*, 109–10
Mushrooms:
  Minnesota hot dish,
    114–15
  stroganoff tots, 33
  tot-stuffed, 63–64
Mussels, in *moules* tots,
  108, 109–10

N

Not your Aunt Sandy's
  po-tot-o salad, 40–41

O

Onion(s):
  caramelized, and bacon,
    tot crust quiche with,
    81–82
  dip, *15*, 17–18
  pickled, 119–20
  vindaloo tots, 12
Oven-baked homemade
  tots, 10

P

Pasta:
  mac and cheese, coated
    in tots and deep-fried,
    66
  mac 'n' tot 'n' cheese,
    119–20, *121*
Pa-tot-as bravas, 31–32
Peppers:
  bibimtot, *96*, 97–99
  spicy romesco sauce,
    55, 56–58
  tot-topped pizza,
    104–7, *105*
  see also Chile peppers
Pickled onions, 119–20
Pickle spears, coated in tots
  and deep-fried, 66
Pico de gallo, 23–24
Pies:
  chicken tot, 111–12, *113*
  shepherd's, with a totty
    top, *116*, 117–18
  sweet po-tot-o, *144*,
    145–46
Pizza, tot-topped,
  104–7, *105*
Pizza tots, 33
Pork:
  bahn mi tots, 33
  meatballs, tot-stuffed,
    with spicy romesco
    sauce, 55, 56–58
  Southern barbecue tots,
    33

  see also Bacon; Ham;
    Sausages
Potatoes. See Tots
Poutine, tots, 27–28

Q

Quiche, tot crust, with
  bacon and caramelized
  onion, 81–82

R

Reuben tots, 33
Rice:
  lomo sal-tot-o, 102–3
  risotto, coated in tots
    and deep-fried, 66
Rosemary truffle tots, 13
Rum-glazed donuts with
  tot-bacon crunch,
  136, 137–39

S

Saag paneer, tots, 100–101
Salads:
  po-tot-o, not your Aunt
    Sally's, 40–41
  tot Caesar, *34*, 35–36
Salted caramel tot cookies,
  147–49, *148*
Sandwiches:
  Kentucky tot hot brown,
    122–23
  monster tot bacon grilled
    cheese, *124*, 125
Sauces:
  cheese, spicy, *15*, 16–17
  chimichurri, *15*, 18–19
  chipotle mayo, *15*, 16
  guacamole, 23–24
  horseradish, *15*, 19
  Mornay, 122–23
  pico de gallo, 23–24
  romesco, spicy, 55,
    56–58
  tomato, 31–32

Sausages:
    breakfast bur-tot-o,
      74–75
    sc-tot-ch eggs, 90–91
    tots and brats, 51–52
    tots-giving stuffing,
      127–28
    tot shakshuka, 83–84,
      85
    tot-stuffed mushrooms,
      63–64
Sc-tot-ch eggs, 90–91
Sesame ginger tots, 14–16
Shakshuka, tot, 83–84, *85*
Shellfish:
    chowder tots, 33
    lobster roll tots, 33
    moules tots, *108,*
      109–10
    shrimp, coated in tots
      and deep-fried, 66
Shepherd's pie with a totty
    top, *116,* 117–18
Shrimp, coated in tots and
    deep-fried, 66
Simple flavor boost for
    tots, 12
Sliders, cheeseburger tot,
    67–68, *69*
Sloppy tots, 33
S'mores tots, 150–52, *151*
Sour cream:
    and caviar, totkes with,
      45–47, *46*
    cheesy tot skins, 61–62
    loaded tots, 25–26
    totchos, *22,* 23–24
Southern barbecue tots,
    33
Spicy cheese sauce, *15,*
    16–17
Spicy romesco sauce, *55,*
    56–58

Spinach:
    -tot dip, 50
    tots saag paneer,
      100–101
Spring rolls, tot-co,
    53–54
Stroganoff tots, 33
Stuffing, tots-giving,
    127–28
Sweet potato(es):
    sweet po-tot-o pie, *144,*
      145–46
    veggie tots, 11

T

Taco tots, 12
Tater tots. *See* Tots
Toad in a tot hole, 92
Toaster pizza tots, 44
Tomato(es):
    green, coated in tots and
      deep-fried, 66
    lomo sal-tot-o, 102–3
    pico de gallo, 23–24
    sauce, 31–32
    shepherd's pie with a
      totty top, *116,* 117–18
    tot shakshuka, 83–84,
      85
    tot-topped pizza, 104–7,
      105
Tortillas:
    breakfast bur-tot-o,
      74–75
    tot migas, 79–80
Tots (homemade):
    broccoli or cauliflower, 11
    flavor boosters, 12
    oven-baked, 10
    recipe for, 9–10
    sweet potatoes or beets,
      11

    veggie, 10–12
    zucchini or apples, 11–12
Tots (store-bought):
    baking directions, 8
    coin-shape, 5–6
    deep-frying directions,
      8
    defrosting, 6
    frozen, buying, 5
    made with sweet
      potatoes, 6
    mini-size, 5
    monster-size, 6
    pan-frying directions, 7
    seasonings, sauces, and
      dips for, 13–19, *15*
    unofficial timeline, 93
Turkey:
    Kentucky tot hot brown,
      122–23
    Minnesota hot dish,
      114–15

V

Vegetables:
    veggie tots, 10–12
    see also specific
      vegetables
Vindaloo tots, 12

W

Waffles, tot-, and chicken,
    86–89, *88*

Z

Zucchini:
    bibimtot, *96,* 97–99
    coated in tots and deep-
      fried, 66
    veggie tots, 11–12